SPIN!

Grammar, Vocabulary, and Writing

A

Genevieve J. Kocienda

Writer: Ellen Balla

Longman

Spin! A Teacher's Guide

Pearson Education, 10 Bank Street, White Plains, NY 10606

Vice president, director of publishing: Allen Ascher
Executive editor: Anne Stribling
Senior development editor: Virginia Bernard
Vice president, director of design and production: Rhea Banker
Executive managing editor: Linda Moser
Production manager: Liza Pleva
Production editor: Sylvia Dare
Art director: Patricia Wosczyk
Director of manufacturing: Patrice Fraccio
Senior manufacturing buyer: Edith Pullman
Cover design: Elizabeth Carlson
Cover art: Mary Jane Begin
Cover photo: © Paul Eekhoff/Masterfile
Text design: Patricia Wosczyk
Text composition: TSI Graphics
Text art: Ellen Appleby

ISBN: 0-13-041982-6

Printed in the United States of America
  2 3 4 5 6 7 8 9 10—BAH—07 06 05 04 03

Contents

Introduction

Spin! is a six-level course that makes learning grammar fun and engaging for students. Each level of **Spin!** contains the following components:

- Student Book
- Teacher's Guide
- Audio Program
- Reproducible Picture Cards

The Student Book

The Student Book contains ten units and five review units. Each unit features an interesting and practical theme within an appropriate vocabulary and grammar context. After the vocabulary is introduced on the first page of the unit, it is used in a series of exercises which explain and practice the grammar point. Each unit also includes a chant and/or a game that allows students to practice the featured vocabulary and grammar in a fun and stimulating way. Review units, which appear after every two units, give students the opportunity to consolidate what they have learned through listening and pronunciation practice. At the back of each Student Book is a picture dictionary to help students develop research and dictionary skills.

The Teacher's Guide

The Teacher's Guide features lesson plans and reduced Student Book pages. The reduced Student Book pages incorporate the answers for each exercise. Each lesson plan consists of a warm-up, an explanation of how to use each page of the Student Book, and games and activities to extend the lesson and reinforce the material learned. The beginning of each lesson includes a guide to grammar, the lesson vocabulary, materials needed, and helpful words and phrases that the teacher can use in the classroom to explain the lesson's activities. The review unit lesson plans also include the recording script of the Audio Program.

Physical movement to develop language skills in activities is adapted in **Spin!** from Total Physical Response (TPR), as developed by James J. Asher. This technique is ideal for students at the early stages of learning, when their capabilities for verbal response are as yet undeveloped. TPR provides both intense listening practice and repeated exposure to basic vocabulary items.

The Audio Program

The Audio Program consists of a recording on cassette or CD. The Audio Program models the vocabulary words, the new grammar patterns, and the chants. Material featured in the Audio Program is indicated in the Student Book by the icon: 🎧.

The Picture Cards

Reproducible Picture Cards of vocabulary words appear at the back of the Teacher's Guide. Sets of Picture Cards can be made for the students as well as the teacher. The Picture Cards are utilized in the lesson activities and can also be used in a variety of ways to enhance classroom learning.

LONGMAN ON THE WEB

Longman.com offers classroom activities, teaching tips, and online resources for teachers of all levels and students of all ages. Visit us for course-specific Companion Websites, our comprehensive online catalogue of all Longman titles, and access to all local Longman websites, offices, and contacts around the world.

Join a global community of teachers and students at **Longman.com**.

Longman English Success offers online courses to give learners flexible, self-paced study options. Developed for distance learning or to complement classroom instruction, courses cover general English, business English, and exam preparation.

For more information visit **EnglishSuccess.com**.

Acknowledgments

The publishers wish to thank the principals, coordinators, teachers, and students of the following schools and institutes. **Mexico City, Mexico:** Centro Educativo Exea, Colegio Martín Luis Guzman, Instituto Ateniense, Centro Escolar Walter Buchana, Colegio Motolinía, Colegio Fernando de Magallanes. **San Luis Potosí, Mexico:** Colegio Teresa Martín, Colegio Guadalupe Victoria, Instituto Kennedy, Colegio Tepeyac, Instituto Hispano Inglés, Colegio Juan de Dios Peza, Instituto Educación Siglo XXI, Instituto Asunción, Instituto Cultural Manuel José Othón, Colegio Miguel de Cervantes. **Caracas, Venezuela:** Colegio Americano, Colegio Claret, Colegio Canigua, Instituto Escuela, Colegio Santiago de León, Colegio Insight, Colegio Los Campitos. **Panama City, Panama:** Instituto Episcopal San Cristobal, Instituto Justo Arosemena, Colegio San Agustin, Colegio Nuestra Señora de Lourdes, Instituto Panamericano. **Guatemala City, Guatemala:** Verbo Christian School, Continental Americano, Lehnsen Roosevelt Bilingual School, Liceo Chapero, Sagrado Corazón, Centro Escobar El Roble, Liceo Bilingüe Las Naciones, Verbo El Valle.

Time Guidelines

	Week 1	Week 2	Week 3	Week 4
Unit 1	Vocabulary Nouns	*Review: Nouns* A/An	*Review: A/An* I am	*Review: as needed* Game
Unit 2	Vocabulary He is/She is	*Review: He is/She is* My Who is he/she?	Chant Game	*Review: Units 1 and 2*
Unit 3	Vocabulary What is it?	*Review: What is it?* Plurals	*Review: Plurals* What are they?	Chant Game
Unit 4	Vocabulary This/That These/Those	*Review: This/That,* *These/Those* Adjectives	Chant Game	*Review: Units 3 and 4*
Unit 5	Vocabulary In, On, Under	*Review: In, On, Under* Where...?	*Review: Where...?* Present Progressive	Chant Game
Unit 6	Vocabulary Is it a... ?	*Review: Is it a...?* Do you have...?	What does he/she have? Chant Game	*Review: Units 5 and 6*
Unit 7	Vocabulary How old...?	*Review: How old...?* His/Her	*Review: His/Her* Whose...?	Chant Game
Unit 8	Vocabulary Does he/she like...?	*Review: Does he/* *she like...?* Do you like...?	Do you want...? Chant Game	*Review: Units 7 and 8*
Unit 9	Vocabulary Can	*Review: Can* Can't	*Review: Can't* Can you...? Can he/she...?	Chant Game
Unit 10	Vocabulary What are you doing?	*Review: What are* *you doing?* What is he/she doing?	How many...? Chant Game	*Review: Units 9 and 10*

Use introduction pages before Unit 1 as appropriate.

Alphabet and Numbers

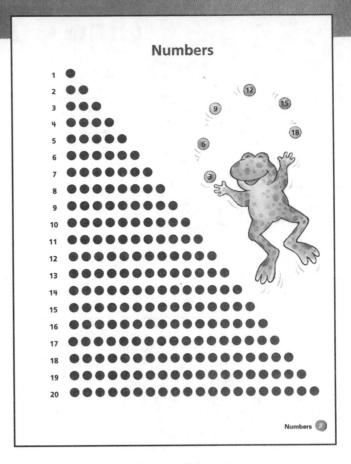

Vocabulary: numbers 1–20, the alphabet a–z, apple, bus, cat, doll, egg, fish, goat, house, inchworm, jacket, king, lemon, map, nut, ostrich, pizza, queen, rabbit, sandwich, tiger, umbrella, van, web, fox, yak, zebra

Lesson Objectives
✓ to say the letters of the alphabet in order and in isolation
✓ to match corresponding pictures to letters of the alphabet
✓ to say the numbers 1–20
✓ to count from 1–20
✓ to match the correct quantity of items to the number

Classroom English
• Find. Say. Draw an X. Listen. Write. Show me. Point to. Circle.

Language Patterns
• It is (A).   • It is (2).

Materials
one set of alphabet cards per student; one number chart per student; index cards with numbers 1–20; index cards with dots from 1–20.

WARMING UP
The Alphabet

Write the alphabet on the board. Sing the alphabet song with students, pointing to each letter. Pause to let students repeat the letter after you. Make alphabet cards with letters and pictures and give one set to each student. Call out letters at random and have students find the letter in their set of alphabet cards.

Numbers

Make number charts with numbers and corresponding pictures and give one to each student. Count from 1–20 as you point to each number and set of pictures. Pause to let students repeat the numbers after you. Write the numbers 1–20 on index cards. Show each card, in order, and count again from 1–20. Show the numbers at random and ask students to name them.

USING PAGE 2

Help students find page 2 in their books. Read each letter and have students point to it in their books. Ask volunteers to identify each picture. Then call out pictures and have volunteers name the corresponding letter from their books. Go to page 99 and have students practice writing the alphabet.

USING PAGE 3

Help students find page 3 in their books. Read each number and have students point to it in their books. Read each number again, and have students count the number of dots chorally. Copy the numbers and dots onto the board. Cover them with a sheet of paper. Point to a row of dots and have volunteers say the correct number. Remove the paper and erase the dots. Call out numbers and ask students to come up and draw the correct number of dots on the board. Do the activity on page 100.

Days of the Week/Months of the Year

Days of the Week

S	M	T	W	Th	F	S
X						

Sunday

Monday

Tuesday

Wednesday

Thursday

Friday

Saturday

Days of the Week

Months of the Year

January

February

March

April

May

June

July

August

September

October

November

December

Months of the Year

Vocabulary: Sunday, Monday, Tuesday, Wednesday, Thursday, Friday, Saturday, January, February, March, April, May, June, July, August, September, October, November, December

Lesson Objectives
✓ to say the days of the week in order and in isolation
✓ to say the months of the year in order and in isolation

Classroom English
• Find. Say. Listen. Write. Show n Point to. Circle.

Language Patterns
• It is (Monday).
• It is (July).

WARMING UP
Days of the Week

Draw a calendar week on the board. Point to and chant the days of the week, pausing after each one so students can repeat. Point to the days at random and ask volunteers to name them.

Months of the Year

Draw a twelve-month calendar on the

such as: *It is Sunday. Maria is watching TV*. Have students repeat. Call out a day and ask volunteers to say a sentence about what the character is doing. Then describe a character and an activity and ask students to name the day.

USING PAGE 5

Help students find page 5 in their books. Invite students to tell what

① use my calendar & Picture Dictionaries

② Model a sentence for each day
  It is Sunday. Maria is watching T.V
  student repeats

③ Call out a day — students· makes sentence about what character is doing

④ Teacher describes a character & an activity
  Ask student to name a day

Colors/Hello!

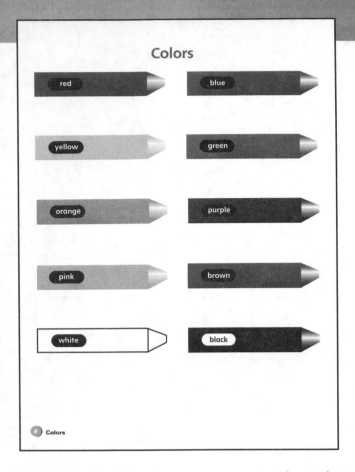

Vocabulary: black, blue, brown, green, hello, orange, pink, purple, red, white, yellow

Lesson Objectives
✓ to say the colors
✓ to greet one another

Classroom English
• Find. Say. Listen. Write. Show me. Point to. Circle.

Language Patterns
• It is (yellow).
• Hello, I'm (Greg).

Materials
crayons; drawing paper; craft sticks; glue; markers; crayons; pencils

WARMING UP
Colors

Use crayons to introduce the colors. Hold up a red crayon and say: *Red. It is red.* Ask students to say this with you. After students are familiar with the first color, add another and ask students to name both. Continue the procedure for all the colors.

Greetings: *Hello. I'm (Alex).*

Make two puppets from drawing paper. Draw faces on each puppet and glue a craft stick to the back. Act out the following conversation and then practice it with students: *Hello. I'm Sue. Hello. I'm Bob.*

USING PAGE 6

Help students find page 6 in their books. Model the activity and give directions: *Show me (red). Color the crayon (red).* Students color each crayon in their books as you identify it.

USING PAGE 7

Help students find page 7 in their books. Play the recording or read the dialogue to the class. Ask students to read along with you. Ask volunteers to take a character's part.

HAVING FUN!
What's Missing?

Place crayons on a table and ask students to name each color. Ask students to close their eyes. Take away one crayon. Then ask students to open their eyes. The student who guesses which color is missing first gets to take away the next crayon.

Find something (red).

Model the activity. Give TPR commands: *Find something (red).* Students walk around the classroom and find something red. If they are able, allow them to identify the object and then say the color.

Unit 1
In the Classroom

Nouns, A/An, I am

Vocabulary: apple, book, classroom, desk, pencil, student, teacher, umbrella

Lesson Objective
✓ to name classroom objects

Classroom English
• Find. Say. Circle. Color. Draw. Show me. Go to. What is it? Who is it?

Materials
• **Realia:** pencil, eraser, book, box, crayons, drawing paper
• **Picture Cards:** apple, book, classroom, desk, pencil, student, teacher, umbrella

WARMING UP

Use classroom objects such as a *pencil, eraser, book*. Place these in a box or bag so students can't see them. Students sit in a circle. Tell students that they are going to play a guessing game. Model the activity. Place your hand in the bag or box and feel what is inside. Shrug your shoulders as if you don't know. Ask: *What is it?* Answer: *(Pencil.)*

Students now play the game. They should save their guesses until everyone has had a turn. If students are able, allow them to guess what the items are in their own language. Then take out each item and model the word by first saying the word and then asking students to repeat it after you. Practice the new vocabulary two or three times before having students complete page 9.

USING PAGE 9

Help students find page 9 in their books. Students identify what they see. Point to items in the picture and ask: *What is it?* Model responses if necessary. Play the recording or read each word. Point to each item and word. Invite students to read with you.

When students are finished, invite them to name the people and objects they see on the page.

HAVING FUN!
Drawing Dictation

Show students how to fold their drawing paper into eight boxes. Help them number the boxes 1–8. Give the following directions and ask students to draw with you:

1. Draw a pencil.
2. Draw an umbrella.
3. Draw a book.
4. Draw an apple.
5. Draw a desk.
6. Draw a student.
7. Draw a classroom.
8. Draw a teacher.

Find It

Place the Picture Cards for the following words faceup on the table: *apple, book, pencil, umbrella, desk, student, classroom, teacher*. Invite students to say the words with you. Now turn over the Picture Cards. Individual students find the pictures when you say: *Find the (book)*. Students keep the cards they find. The student with the most cards at the end of the game wins.

Vocabulary: apple, book, classroom, desk, pencil, student, teacher, umbrella

Lesson Objective
✓ to write and categorize nouns

Classroom English
• Find. Say. Color. Show me. Go to.

Materials
• drawing paper, glue, scissors, magazines
• **Realia:** desk, eraser, pencil, umbrella
• **Picture Cards:** boy, classroom, desk, girl, pencil, school, student, teacher, umbrella

WARMING UP

Help students find different items in the classroom. Say: *Find a desk.* Model by pointing to a desk. Ask them: *What is it?* Model the response: *Desk.* Continue with the words: *boy, classroom, desk, eraser, girl, pencil, student, teacher, umbrella.*

Use the Picture Cards to categorize the people. Hold up the Picture Card for *boy* and model: *boy, person.* Students repeat after you. Continue with the words and Picture Cards *girl, student, teacher.* Place these in a pile in front of students and say: *person.*

Use the same procedure to help students categorize places and things. Make category piles. Say each word with them and then model the category names *place* and *thing.* Students should repeat after you.

Ahead of time, draw a stick figure, a chair and a board, and a desk on the board. Label each picture with its name and category: *student/person, classroom/place, desk/thing.* Write the word *noun* above your pictures. Point to the word *noun* and read it with students. Now identify each picture and ask them to repeat whether it is a *person, place,* or *thing.*

Nouns

A noun is a person, place, or thing.

Person	Place	Thing
student	classroom	desk

Point and write.

1. place

classroom

2. thing

desk

3. person

student

Show students how to trace each word and then invite them to come up and trace the words on the board.

USING PAGE 10

Help students find page 10 in their books. Play the recording or read the Grammar Box and point to the pictures. Students repeat after you. Ask students to repeat the definition of a noun and point to the three pictures in the box, naming the pictures and saying, *person, place,* or *thing.*

Now read the directions for the writing activity on this page and instruct students to follow along. Tell them that they will be pointing to and tracing the words. Begin by pointing

to the picture of the classroom and having them repeat the word after you. Point to the word *place* above it and ask them to say it with you. Continue with numbers 2 and 3. Students should trace the words. As they are working, walk around and ask them to point to the words and read individually for you. Ask them to categorize the words as either a *person, place,* or *thing.*

Look and write.

teacher   boy   school   pencil

playground   umbrella   classroom

eraser   girl

Person	Place	Thing
teacher	school	eraser
boy	playground	umbrella
girl	classroom	pencil

Nouns, A/An, I am 11

USING PAGE 11

Help students find page 11 in their books. Read the directions as students follow along. Tell them that they are going to be writing the words in the correct categories. Begin by pointing to the pictures and reading each word. Ask them to repeat after you. Then ask: *Person? Place? Thing?* Focus their attention on the second half of the page. Point to and read each category heading with students. Point to the word *teacher* in the first column and read it with them. Point to the category heading *Person* and ask them to read it with you. Tell them that they are going to find all the pictures that show people. Point to the *boy* and ask: *Person?* Prompt them to answer: *Yes.* Show them how to write the word *boy* on the line in

the first column. Point to the word *school.* Ask: *Person?* Prompt them to answer: *No.* Continue in this manner, having them identify all the people and model how to write them in the first column.

Use the same procedure for the next two columns, *Place* and *Thing.* When students have completed the activity, invite them to read words from each column and to point to the corresponding picture.

HAVING FUN!
Sorting

Use the Picture Cards for this unit. Draw a stick picture of a person on the board and label it *person.* Draw a picture of a book on the board and label it *thing.* Draw a picture of a swing and a tree and label it *place.*

Quickly review the vocabulary with students by showing them the Picture Cards and having them tell what they see. Model the words if necessary. Then ask: *Person? Place? Thing?* Ask them to come up and place the picture in the correct category. This can be played in teams. The team with the most correct answers wins.

Making Collages

If possible, bring in old magazines that students can cut. Students should cut out pictures of persons, places, and things and glue them on three different pieces of drawing paper. Students should label their collages *person, place,* or *thing.* Model how to write these words if necessary. You can do one collage a day. When their collages are finished, invite students to come up, talk about their pictures, and tell if they are *persons, places,* or *things.* Display the collages for everyone to enjoy.

Find It

Place the Picture Cards in obvious places around the room. Tell students to find all the pictures. Students can work in teams or groups. After all the pictures have been found, ask them to sit in a circle, identify each picture, and tell if it is a *person, place,* or *thing.* Prompt them with questions: *What is it? Person? Place? Thing?*

What's Missing?

Place the Picture Cards for this lesson on the floor or a table in front of students. Review the vocabulary by asking: *What is it? (School). Who is it? (Teacher).* Turn over the Picture Cards. Motion for students to close their eyes and take away one of the cards. Ask them to open their eyes and then point to the empty space. Hold up the Picture Card so they cannot see it. Ask: *What is it?* The student who guesses correctly gets to take away the next card while the rest of the class closes their eyes.

Vocabulary: apple, book, classroom, desk, eraser, pencil, school, student, teacher, umbrella

Lesson Objectives
✓ to identify classroom objects and people

✓ to learn the rule for using *a* and *an*

✓ to use *a* and *an* with nouns when speaking and writing

Classroom English
• Say. Circle. Write. What is it?

Language Patterns
• a (book)

• an (eraser)

Materials
• letters of the alphabet written on small slips of paper, magazines

• index cards: draw two of each picture: apple, book, boy, classroom, desk, eraser, girl, playground, school, teacher, umbrella

• a bag

• **Realia:** apple, book, eraser, pencil

• **Picture Cards:** apple, book, school, student, teacher, umbrella

WARMING UP

If possible, show students a real apple and a real book. Model and ask students to repeat: *A book. An apple.* Emphasize the words *a* and *an* to help students see that these words are different.

Present the words in categories. Model and ask students to repeat: *A book. A school. A student. A teacher. A classroom. A desk. A pencil.* Place the Picture Cards for these words in a pile in front of students. Model and ask students to repeat: *An apple. An eraser. An umbrella.* Emphasize the word *an* to help them see that it is different from the first set of words.

Write the alphabet on the board ahead of time. Say: *A book. An apple.*

Ask students to repeat as you hold up each picture or item. Write the words *book* and *apple* on the board. Underline the first letter in each word. Tell students that the word *apple* begins with a vowel. Say the alphabet with the class and circle the vowels as you say them. Tell students that when words begin with a vowel sound, we say *an.* Now point to the word *book* and the letter *b* at the beginning of the word. Explain that this is a consonant. Say only the consonants as you point to each letter. Tell students that when a word begins with a consonant sound, we say *a.*

Write *a* and *an* on the board and read these words with students. Show the picture for the word *book* and write the word on the board with a line

before it. Ask students what letter *book* begins with and if it is a vowel or a consonant. Prompt them to respond that the word begins with the letter *b* and that it is a consonant. Write *a* on the line before the word *book.* Read it with students. Continue with the words *school, apple, umbrella,* writing either *a* or *an* before each word.

USING PAGE 12

Help students find page 12 in their books. Play the recording or read the Grammar Box and point to the pictures. Students should point to and repeat the rules after you. Point to each picture and read the words. Students follow along and read with you.

Point to the picture at the bottom of the page. Ask: *What is it?* Ask

Look and circle.

1. a / **an** apple

2. **a** / an book

3. **a** / an classroom

4. a / **an** eraser

5. a / **an** umbrella

6. **a** / an teacher

7. **a** / an pencil

8. **a** / an desk

students to repeat after you: *a teacher, a student, an apple.* Remind them that *apple* begins with a vowel sound and we say *an. Teacher* and *student* begin with consonant sounds, so we say *a.* Read the directions and ask students to follow along. Show them how to trace the words.

Using page 13

Help students find page 13 in their books. Read the directions as they follow along. Point to the apple and ask: *What is it?* Model the response: *An apple.* Point to the words *a* and *an* and read them with students. Students trace the circle around the word *an.* Read the correct response with them. Continue with the word *book.* Ask: *What is it?* Help them

respond: *A book.* Point to the words *a* and *an* and read them with the class. Show them how to circle the word *a* for *book.* Continue in this manner, having students circle *a* or *an* for each word and picture.

When students are finished, invite them to name the people and objects they see on the page.

Having Fun!
Letter Sort

Write the letters of the alphabet on slips of paper ahead of time and mix them up. Write the words *Consonant* and *Vowel* on the board. Read these words with students. Invite them to come up, choose a letter, and tell if it is a consonant or vowel. Ask them to place it under the correct category

word on the board. You can play this in teams.

Word Sort

Write the words *a* and *an* on the board and read them with students. Show a picture of a book. Write the word *book* on the board and ask students to read chorally. Ask them if this word begins with a vowel or a consonant. Prompt them to answer that it begins with the consonant *b.* Show them how to put the picture under the word *a* on the board. Continue the activity, using the following words: *apple, book, boy, classroom, desk, eraser, girl, pencil, playground, school, student, teacher, umbrella.* As students are sorting the words, ask them if the picture shows a person, place, or thing.

Match It

Draw two of each picture ahead of time: *apple, book, boy, classroom, desk, girl, pencil, playground, school, student, teacher, umbrella.* Quickly review each word with students. Show the pictures and ask: *What is it?* Model the response: *A (book). An (apple).*

Now place all the pictures facedown on the table. Turn over two pictures and name each picture. If the pictures match, keep them. If they do not, the turn goes to the student on your right. Encourage students to use *a* and *an.* Ask if the pictures show a person, place, or thing. Continue playing until all the matches have been found.

A and *An* Pictures

Bring in old magazines. Show students how to fold a piece of drawing paper in half. Label one side *a* and the other side *an.* Students cut out pictures from the magazines that fit these categories. Show them a finished project before they begin and ask them to talk about the pictures you have used.

Vocabulary: boy, girl, student, teacher

Lesson Objective
✓ to use *I am*

Classroom English
• Draw. Say. Write.

Language Pattern
• I am a (student).

Materials
• crayons, pencils, paper
• paper puppet faces (boy and girl)
• **Picture Cards:** boy, girl, student, teacher

WARMING UP

Make simple boy and girl puppets by drawing faces on paper. Hold up the boy in front of your face and say: *I am a boy.* Invite the boys to stand and repeat. Now hold up the girl in front of your face and say: *I am a girl.* Invite the girls to stand and repeat. Hold up Picture Cards of the boy and girl. Say: *I am a student.* Ask students to stand and repeat after you. Point to yourself and say: *I am a teacher.*

Say one of these sentences: *I am a student. I am a boy. I am a girl. I am a teacher.* If the sentence applies to them, students should stand and repeat it. Write the following sentences on the board in one column: *I am a student. I am a boy. I am a girl. I am a teacher.* In another column draw a simple picture for each sentence. Read and point to each word as students repeat. Show how to find the picture in the other column that matches the sentence. Invite a student to draw a line from the sentence to the picture. Continue with all of the sentences.

USING PAGE 14

Help students find page 14 in their books. Play the recording or read the Grammar Box, and ask students to

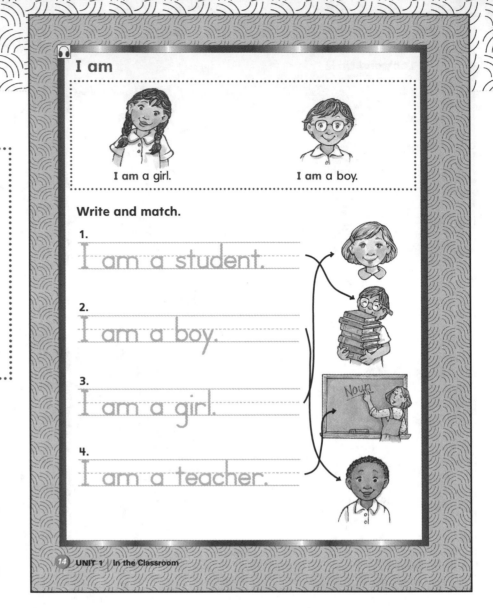

I am

I am a girl.   I am a boy.

Write and match.

1. I am a student.

2. I am a boy.

3. I am a girl.

4. I am a teacher.

repeat. Tell them that we use the words *I am* when we talk about ourselves. Read each sentence and ask the class to repeat.

Read the directions for the writing activity as students follow along. As you read the first sentence, point to each word and ask the class to repeat. Show them how to find the picture that goes with the sentence and to draw a line to connect them. Continue matching the sentences to the pictures. When finished, show students how to trace the words in each sentence.

HAVING FUN!
Draw and Say

Give each student a piece of drawing paper. Write: *I am* on the board and

read it chorally. Show students how to write *I am (their name)* at the bottom of their papers. Now ask them to draw a picture of themselves. When finished, students sit in a circle and tell who they are: *I am (Greg).*

I Am

Students form a line at the front of the classroom. Point to yourself and say: *I am (Mrs. Lewis).* Point to the student next to you and help him or her respond: *I am (Alex).* Show this student how to point to the next person in line, who then says who he or she is. Continue until everyone has had a turn.

Vocabulary: apple, book, boy, classroom, desk, eraser, girl, pencil, playground, school, student, teacher, umbrella

Lesson Objectives
✓ to review classroom object vocabulary
✓ to review that nouns name a *person*, *place* or *thing*

Classroom English
• Draw. Show me. Find. Say. What is it?

Language Patterns
• a (student)
• an (umbrella)

Materials
• **Realia:** eraser, book, apple, desk, pencil
• **Picture Cards:** apple, book, boy, classroom, desk, girl, pencil, school, student, teacher, umbrella

WARMING UP

Show students the Picture Cards for: *teacher, boy, girl, student.* Ask them to identify each one. Ask: *Who is it?* Help students respond: *A (boy).* Ask: *Person? Place? Thing?* After students respond, write the word *Person* on the board and read it with them. Place these pictures under this heading.

Show them pictures or realia for: *book, apple, desk, eraser, pencil.* Ask: *What is it?* Help them respond: *A (desk).* If necessary, remind them when to use *a* and *an.* After they answer, write the word *Thing* on the board and read it with the class. Place the Picture Cards or realia under this heading.

Show the class the Picture Cards for *school and classroom.* Ask: *What is it?* After they respond, write the word *Place* on the board and place the pictures under this heading.

Draw.

Person

Thing

Place

Nouns, A/An, I am 15

USING PAGE 15

Help students find page 15 in their books. Read the directions as students follow along. Read the titles that are in each box and ask students to read with you. Show them how to draw pictures for a person, place, or thing in the corresponding boxes.

HAVING FUN!
Show Me

Model responses such as: *A book. An eraser.* Ask if the pictures show a person, place, or thing. Play a Show Me game with them.

Model the activity. Invite two students to come up. Say: *Show me a person.* Students point to a person in the room and tell who it is. Continue the

game by having them point to persons, places, and things. They can point to the *school* and the *classroom* when you say *Point to a place.*

Find It

Use the Picture Cards for these words: *apple, book, boy, classroom, desk, eraser, girl, pencil, school, student, teacher, umbrella.* Students should sit in a circle on the floor. Place the pictures on the floor faceup. Quickly review the words with them. As they respond, encourage them to use *a* and *an* correctly. Ask: *Person? Place? Thing?* Turn the cards over. Say: *Find the (boy).* The student on your right begins by turning over one card. If he or she finds the (boy), he or she keeps it. Continue playing until all the pictures have been found.

Vocabulary: apple, eraser, classroom, girl, playground, school, teacher, umbrella

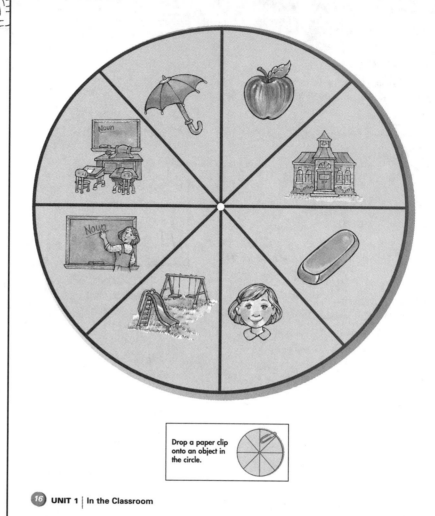

What is it?

Drop a paper clip onto an object in the circle.

WARMING UP

Review the vocabulary: *apple, eraser, classroom, girl, playground, school, teacher, umbrella.* Hold up a Picture Card for each word and ask: *What is it? Who is it?* Encourage students to use *a* and *an* correctly: *A boy. An apple.*

USING PAGE 16
Person, Place, or Thing

Help students find page 16 in their books. Show them the game board. Demonstrate how to drop a paper clip onto the game board. Each student gets a turn. Students name the item or person and tell if it is a person, place, or thing. Students earn one point for each correct answer. The student with the most points at the end of the game wins. This can be played in groups or as a class.

A and *An*

Point out the game board. Show students how to drop a paper clip onto the game board. Each student gets a turn. Students name the item and use *a* or *an.* Students earn one point for each correct response. The student with the most points at the end of the game wins. This can be played in groups or as a class.

EXTENSION
Card Game

Draw two of each picture on index cards: *apple, book, boy, classroom, desk, eraser, girl, pencil, school, student, teacher, umbrella.* Model the game. Deal out all the cards to students. Show students how to hold

their cards so other students cannot see their cards. Students place all matches on the table and name the pictures. Remind them to use *a* and *an* when responding. After they have placed down all their pairs, they take turns choosing a card from the student on their right. If students get a match, they place it on the table and name the picture. Continue having them choose cards from each other until all the cards have been paired. The student with the most pairs wins. While playing, students can also tell if the pictures show a person, place, or thing.

Unit 2
My Family

He is/She is, My, Who is he/she?

Vocabulary: brother, family, father, grandfather, grandmother, he, me, mother, she, sister

Lesson Objectives
✓ to talk about one's family
✓ to name family members
✓ to identify and trace the words *he* and *she*

Classroom English
• Find. Say. Circle. Draw. Write. Read. Show me. What is it? Who is he? Who is she?

Language Patterns
• He is a (brother).
• She is a (mother).

Materials
• crayons, drawing paper, index cards with the words *he* and *she* (one *he* index card for each boy and one *she* index card for each girl)
• **Realia:** picture of a family that shows a mother, father, sister, brother, grandmother, grandfather
• **Picture Cards:** grandfather, grandmother, mother, father, sister, brother

My Family

He is/She is, My, Who is he/she? 17

WARMING UP

Show students a picture of a family that includes a mother, father, sister, brother, grandmother, and grandfather. Ask them to tell what they see. Allow them to answer using whatever English they know or their native language.

Show students the Picture Cards for the following words: *mother, father, grandmother, grandfather, sister, brother.* Say each word and ask them to repeat. After you have done this a few times and students are comfortable with the vocabulary, model complete sentences. First model sentences with *he.* Then model sentences with *she.* For example: *She*

is a mother. She is a sister. She is a grandmother.* Students repeat as you hold up each picture. Allow them to practice a few times before you continue with: *He is a father. He is a grandfather. He is a brother.*

Write *She is a mother.* on the board and read it with students. Ask a volunteer to find the picture of the mother and place it next to the sentence. Invite a student to come up and trace the words *She is.* Continue with other examples that use this pattern: *She is a grandmother. He is a brother. He is a father.*

USING PAGE 17

Help students find page 17 in their books. Allow them to talk about the

pictures and encourage them to use the unit vocabulary. Do a Show Me activity. Say sentences such as: *Show me a grandfather.* Model pointing to the picture and saying the word *(grandfather).* Continue with other vocabulary.

Point to the pictures and say the words or play the recording. Ask students to point and repeat chorally. Then ask individual students to name the people. Ask: *Who is he? Who is she?* Students answer with the vocabulary: *(grandfather).*

Do a listening activity with students. Hold up a (green) crayon and say: *Show me a (green) crayon. Circle grandmother.* Continue circling the other pictures with different colored crayons.

USING PAGE 18

Help students find page 18 in their books. Point to the words at the top of the page and play the recording or read them with students. Ask them to talk about the pictures. Encourage them to use the key vocabulary from this unit. Point to the pictures for each sentence and read them. Ask students to read with you. Tell them that when we talk about a girl we use the word *she*. When we talk about a boy we use the word *he*.

Point to number 1. Allow students to talk about the picture. Read the sentence and point to the brother in the picture. Show students how to trace the sentence. Students now trace the words. When they are finished, read the sentence chorally. Complete the page with them and then read chorally.

HAVING FUN!
Hunting Game: *He* and *She*

Write the words *he* and *she* on index cards ahead of time. There should be one *he* card for each boy and one *she* card for each girl. Hide the cards in obvious places around the classroom. Model the activity. Boys hunt for the word *he*. Girls hunt for the word *she*. Students can work with a buddy. When they find their word, ask them to sit in a circle. When everyone is sitting, place the Picture Cards for *mother, father, grandfather, grandmother, sister,* and *brother* on the floor in front of them. Ask them to tell who everyone is. Hold up an index card with the word *he* and say: *He is a (father)*. Hold up an index card with the word *she* and model the sentence: *She is a (mother)*. Invite individual students to stand up, read their word, and point to the picture that goes with it. More advanced students can say the complete sentence.

He is/She is

He is a grandfather.   She is a sister.

Point and write.

1. He is a brother.
2. She is a mother.
3. He is a father.
4. She is a grandmother.

He and *She* Sorting

Ahead of time, write the words *he* and *she* on the board above two columns. Read them with students. Hold up one of the Picture Cards for this unit and ask: *He? She?* After students have replied, place the picture in the correct column. Continue with the rest of the Picture Cards, asking students to sort them.

What's Missing?

Place the Picture Cards for this unit on the floor or a table in front of students. Review them by modeling each word and asking students to repeat. Ask students to close their eyes. Take away one card. Ask them to open their eyes and say: *Who?*

Shrug your shoulders and point to the space where the card was. Students now try to guess who's missing. The student who guesses correctly first gets to take away the next card.

Who is he? Who is she?

Place the Picture Cards for this unit in a stack, without letting students see which one is on top. Place a piece of paper on top of the first picture. Ask: *Who is he/she?* Slowly pull up the piece of paper, showing a little bit of the picture. Continue to pull up the paper a little at a time until someone can guess who it is. The student who guesses correctly first keeps the card. The student with the most cards wins.

Vocabulary: brother, family, father, grandfather, grandmother, he, mother, my, she, sister

Lesson Objectives

✓ to talk about one's family

✓ to name family members

✓ to identify and trace the words *he* and *she*

✓ to use *my*

Classroom English

• Find. Say. Color. Draw. Write. Show me. What is it? Who is he? Who is she?

Language Patterns

• He is my (brother).

• She is my (mother).

Materials

• index cards with the words: *it, a, my, he, she, is, me*; bingo grids with nine spaces, one for each student; bingo markers

• **Picture Cards:** brother, sister, mother, father, grandmother, grandfather

My

My shows belonging.

He is my brother.

She is my sister.

Draw.

My Family

He is/She is, My, Who is he/she? 19

WARMING UP

Review the key vocabulary with students. Say each word and ask them to repeat. After you have practiced the words in isolation, invite them to say complete sentences. Model sentences for students. For example: *She is a mother.* Now ask students to close their eyes. Place a Picture Card behind your back. Students open their eyes and you ask: *Who is (he/she)?* The student who guesses correctly first gets to hold the next picture behind his or her back.

Now draw a picture of your family on the board. As you are drawing, ask students to guess who it is. When your picture is finished, model sentences such as: *She is my sister.* As you say each sentence, point first to the person in your picture. Then when you say the word *my*, point to yourself. Invite students to practice these sentences with you.

USING PAGE 19

Help students find page 19 in their books. Point to the pictures and ask them to tell you who they see. Point to the word *My* at the top of the page and read it for students. Ask them to read with you. Point to each word as you read the sentences or play the recording and invite students to point and repeat. Read the directions for the activity and ask them to read with you. Model how to complete this page. Refer students back to the picture you drew in the warm-up.

Write *My Family* under your picture and read with students. Identify all the people in your picture and use sentences such as: *He is my father.* Students draw pictures of their families. When their pictures are finished, invite students to share their work with the rest of the class. Encourage them to use the language presented on this page.

USING PAGE 20

Help students find page 20 in their books. Point to each picture and ask them to tell who they see. Read the first sentence and ask them to read with you. Help them complete the sentence orally and then help them find the correct word that finishes the sentence. Show them how to circle the word and how to write it on the line. Complete the page with students and read chorally.

HAVING FUN!
Reading Fun

Write the following words on index cards, making two of each: *it, a, my, he, she, is, me.* Read each word and ask students to read with you. Place the index cards faceup on a table and ask for volunteers to read. Now turn the cards facedown. Students take turns turning over two cards. Encourage students to read the words as they turn over the cards. If the words match, they keep the pair. The student with the most pairs wins.

Find It

Model the activity. Place the Picture Cards for these words in obvious places around the classroom: *grandfather, grandmother, mother, father, brother, sister.* Say: *Find a (grandmother).* Students look around the room and point to the picture. Encourage them to say: *(She) is a (grandmother).*

Show Me

Ask students to sit in a circle. Place the Picture Cards for the following words on the floor: *grandfather, grandmother, mother, father, brother, sister.* Review the vocabulary by asking: *Who is (he/she)?* Model responses if necessary and ask students to repeat. Now invite two

Circle and write.

My family.

1. He is my brother.
   (brother)   mother

2. She is my grandmother.
   (grandmother)   father

3. He is my father
   sister   (father)

4. She is my sister
   brother   (sister)

5. He is my grandfather
   (grandfather)   mother

students to sit in front of the cards. Say: *Show me a (grandmother).* The student who points to the correct picture first wins.

Word Bingo

Write these words on a set of index cards ahead of time: *it, my, a, he, she, is, me.* Prepare bingo grids for students ahead of time. Bingo grids should have nine spaces. Write two free spaces on each grid. Help the students write the words on their grids: *it, a, my, he, she, is, me.* Encourage them to write the words in random order so each bingo grid is different. Show students how to place a marker on the free spaces. Call out the words at random and show students how to place a marker on

the word you call. Three in a row wins.

Listen

Place the vocabulary Picture Cards on the board. Ask students to form a line from the front to the back of the room. Model the activity. Whisper one of the vocabulary words to the first student. Motion for this student to whisper it to the next student in line. Students continue whispering the word until the last student is reached. The last student comes up to the board, says the word, then points to the corresponding Picture Card. Encourage students to say a complete sentence: *(He) is a (grandfather).*

Vocabulary: brother, father, grandfather, grandmother, mother, my, sister

Lesson Objectives
✓ to talk about one's family
✓ to name family members
✓ to use *who*

Classroom English
• Say. Circle. Write. What is it? Who is he? Who is she?

Language Patterns
• Who is he? He is my (grandfather).
• Who is she? She is my (sister).

Materials
• pictures of students' families (brought from home)
• **Picture Cards:** mother, father, sister, brother, grandmother, grandfather, book, school, classroom, desk, pencil

WARMING UP

Use the vocabulary Picture Cards for this unit: *grandmother, grandfather, mother, father, sister, brother.* Review vocabulary. Ask: *Who is he/she?* Model responses: *(He) is a (father).* Hold up the picture of the (mother) and ask: *Who is (she)?* Motion for students to repeat the question. Offer the response: *She is a mother.* Hold up the rest of the Picture Cards. Model the question: *Who is he/she?* and ask students to ask you the question. Offer the correct responses. Now ask students to sit in a circle. Give the student on your right a Picture Card. Model the question: *Who is he/she?* Students respond with: *(He) is a (father).* Students pass the card to each other and ask and answer the question. Model if necessary.

Place the Picture Card for *grandfather* on the board and write the question and answer next to the Picture Card: *Who is he? He is a grandfather.* Now show students the Picture Card for

mother. Write the question and answer next to this Picture Card: *Who is she? She is a mother.* Show students how to trace the word *Who* in each question. Ask students to come up and trace this word.

Place the Picture Card for *mother* on the board. Write the following on the board next to the picture: _____ *is she?* _____ _____ _____ *mother.* Ask the question and point to each blank space and word. Say the question: *Who is she?* Help students fill in the missing word *who* to complete the question. Point to each space and ask the students to repeat the response: *She is a mother.* Show them how to write the missing words to complete the response. Read the question and answer and ask

students to repeat. Continue with sentences that follow this pattern.

USING PAGE 21

Help students find page 21 in their books. Point to the pictures in the Grammar Box and ask: *Who is he/she?* Model responses if necessary. Play the recording or read the question and answer for each picture and ask students to repeat. Tell students that when we ask a question about a person we use the question word *who.*

Point to the picture for number 1 and ask students to do the same. Ask: *Who is he?* Help them respond: *He is my father.* Now read the question and answer. Ask them to read with you. After you read each sentence with them, show them how to trace the words. Complete the page with students. Invite pairs of students to read the questions and answers.

USING PAGE 22

Help students find page 22 in their books. Read the directions and ask them to read with you. Point to each picture and ask them to tell what they see. Point to number 1 and ask: *Who is he?* Model the response and ask them to repeat: *He is my father.* Show them how to fill in the missing words in the questions and answers. Show them how to draw a line to match the question and answer to the illustration. Complete the page with the students. When the page is complete, read each question and answer chorally.

HAVING FUN!
Write *Who* or *What*

Write the words *Who* and *What* on the board and read them with students. Show them a Picture Card from Unit 1 or Unit 2. Review the words with students by asking either *Who is he?*, *Who is she?*, or *What is it?* Hold up one of the Picture Cards and ask students: *Who? What?* Place the Picture Card on the board and show them how to write the correct word, *who/what* next to the Picture Card.

Ask Each Other

Model the activity. Use Picture Cards from Units 1 and 2. Hold up the picture of the mother and ask: *Who is she?* Model the response: *She is a mother.* Now ask two students to come up. One student asks the question and one student responds. Continue the activity using nouns for

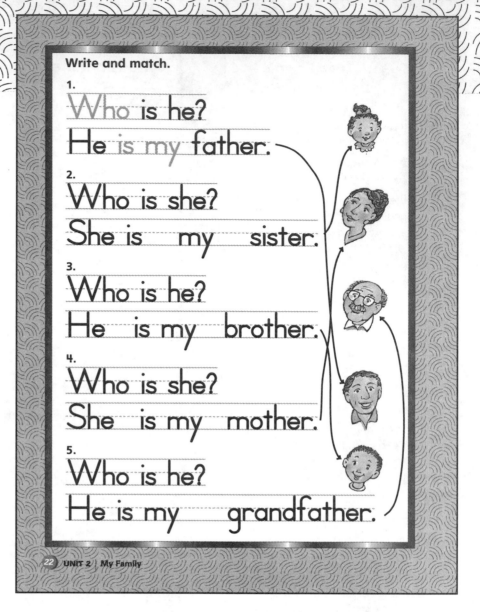

Write and match.

1. Who is he?
   He is my father.
2. Who is she?
   She is my sister.
3. Who is he?
   He is my brother.
4. Who is she?
   She is my mother.
5. Who is he?
   He is my grandfather.

22 UNIT 2 | My Family

people. Remind students that we use the question word *who* for people.

Who is Missing?

Use Picture Cards from Units 1 and 2. Review the questions and responses with students: *Who is (he)? He is a (brother).* Place the Picture Cards on the floor in front of students. Ask them to close their eyes. Take one Picture Card away. Ask: *Who?* and point to the space where you took away the card. The student who answers correctly first gets to take away the next card and ask the question. Model the questions for students if necessary.

My Family Pictures

Invite students to bring in pictures of their families. Begin by asking them to sit in a circle. Show a picture of your family and model sentences such as: *He is my father. She is my mother.* Now invite students to come up and share their photos. Prompt them with the questions: *Who is he? Who is she?*

Vocabulary: brother, father, grandfather, grandmother, mother, sister

Lesson Objectives
✓ to talk about one's family
✓ to say a chant about the family
✓ to complete a maze

Classroom English
• Say. Show me. Find. Draw a line.

Language Patterns
• Who is he? He's my (father).
• Who is she? She's my (grandmother).
• Yes, he is. Yes, she is.

Materials
• crayons, pencils, drawing paper
• **Picture Cards:** brother, sister, father, mother, grandmother, grandfather

USING PAGE 23

Display Picture Cards for *brother, sister, father,* and *mother.* Point to each Picture Card and ask: *Who is he/she?* Model responses if necessary. Help students find page 23 in their books. Read the first four lines of the chant. Point to each word as you read, and ask students to follow along. Refer to the corresponding Picture Cards as you are reading the question and answer.

Model the rest of the chant. Read four lines at a time and point to each word as you read. Invite students to read the chant with you. As you say each line, point to each word and ask students to do the same. Now play the recording and chant with the students.

Divide the class into two groups: one to ask the question and one to respond. Model the question for group 1 and ask students to repeat as they point to each word in the chant. Now motion for group 2 to read the response as they point to each word.

🎧 Chant.

Who is he?
He's my brother.
Yes, he is.
Yes, he is.

Who is she?
She's my sister.
Yes, she is.
Yes, she is.

Who is he?
He's my father.
Yes, he is.
Yes, he is.

Who is she?
She's my mother.
Yes, she is.
Yes, she is.

He's = He is
She's = She is

He is/She is, My, Who is he/she? 23

As students read, point to the corresponding Picture Card.

Invite pairs of students to read the chant, one to ask the question and one to offer the response.

Using Page 24

Help students find page 24 in their books. Point to each picture in the maze and ask: *Who is he/she?* Model responses if necessary. Read the directions and ask students to read with you. Show them how to complete the maze with their fingers. Students now complete the maze with a crayon or pencil. When they are finished, ask them to work in pairs. Students ask and answer: *Who is he/she? (He) is a (grandfather).*

Having Fun!
Who Pictures

Ahead of time, draw a picture of a mother on a piece of drawing paper. Below the picture, write the question: *Who is she?* Show students the completed paper to use as a model. Talk about who is in your picture. Give each student a piece of drawing paper. Show them how to write the question: *Who is he?* or *Who is she?* at the bottom of their papers, and then to draw a response to the question. When students are finished, ask them to sit in a circle. They can ask and answer: *Who is he/she? (He) is a (grandfather).*

24 · UNIT 2 | My Family

Units 1 & 2
Review

Vocabulary: apple, blue, boy, brown, classroom, father, girl, grandfather, grandmother, green, mother, orange, pencil, pink, playground, red, sister, student, teacher, umbrella

Review Objectives
✓ to name classroom objects
✓ to name family members and other people
✓ to recognize and say colors

Classroom English
• Listen. Check. Color. Point. Say.
• It is a (pencil). (He/She) is a teacher.

Language Patterns
• It is a (pencil).
• (He/She) is a teacher.

Materials
• crayons
• **Realia:** umbrella, apple, pencil
• **Picture Cards:** student, teacher, sister, girl, grandmother, father, umbrella, apple, classroom, pencil, boy, playground

WARMING UP

Review the vocabulary words from Units 1 and 2 with students. Use the Picture Cards or realia. Ask: *What is it?* Invite students to use a complete sentence when answering: *It is a (pencil).*

Tape two Picture Cards to the board and draw a box under each Picture Card. Ask children to identify each picture. Ask: *What is it?* Students should answer using a complete sentence: *It is a (pencil).* Now identify only one picture by saying: *It is a (pencil).* Place a check in the box under this Picture Card. Explain to students that as they complete the review pages, they should listen and check the correct picture. Provide additional examples and invite students to check the correct box for the Picture Card you name.

Tape one Picture Card to the board and write *yes* and *no* under the Picture Card. Draw a small box next to the words *yes* and *no*. Say *It is a (pencil).* and point to the Picture Card. Students should verify if the sentence you said is correct or incorrect. If it is correct, place a check in the *yes* box. If the sentence is incorrect, place a check in the *no* box. Provide additional examples and invite students to come up and check the correct box.

If you feel students need to practice exercises that are similar to those presented in the Review Units, use exercises like the two previous exercises so students can practice checking boxes and pictures that go with stated sentences and words.

Review: Units 1 and 2

Vocabulary
🎧 **A. Listen and check.**

Nouns
🎧 **B. Listen and check.**

Review | Units 1 and 2 ·25·

A. 1. student   2. umbrella   3. apple   4. classroom

B. 1. apple   2. teacher   3. umbrella   4. pencil   5. boy   6. playground

Review | Units 1 and 2   25

Review the pronouns *he* and *she* with students. Hold up a Picture Card of a person: *brother, sister, mother, grandfather, teacher, father.* Ask students to tell you which pronoun they should use, *he* or *she*. Show each Picture Card again and ask students to tell you who they see and to use a complete sentence: *He is a (grandfather).*

USING PAGE 25

Help students find page 25 in their books. Help students find Exercise A. Read the directions and ask them to follow along. Point to each picture and ask students to say the words with you. Explain to students that they should check the picture that goes with the word that they hear. Play the recording or read the audioscript for students. Students check the correct picture.

Help students find Exercise B. Read the directions and ask them to follow along. Point to the picture and ask students to repeat each word after you. Explain to students that they should check the word *yes* or *no,* depending on the word that is said. Play the recording or read the audioscript. Students check either the *yes* or *no* box after the sentence is read.

USING PAGE 26

Help students find page 26 in their books. Help students find Exercise C. Read the directions and ask them to

Review: Units 1 and 2

He is/She is
C. Listen and color. Then point and say.

1. Blue
2. Green
3. Pink
4. Orange
5. Red
6. Brown

D. Listen, point, and say.

1. mother
2. sister
3. brother
4. grandfather
5. teacher
6. father

26 Review | Units 1 and 2

follow along. Explain to students that they should listen and color the pictures. Play the recording or read the audioscript for students. Students color the pictures according to the directions. Read the audioscript or play the recording again. This time students point to the appropriate picture and repeat.

Help students find Exercise D. Read the directions and ask them to follow along. Explain that they should listen, point to the picture, and then say the word. Play the recording or read the audioscript for students.

AUDIOSCRIPT

C. 1. Color the student blue.
2. Color the teacher green.
3. Color the sister pink.
4. Color the girl orange.
5. Color the grandmother red.
6. Color the father brown.

1. He is a student.
2. She is a teacher.
3. She is a sister.
4. She is a girl.
5. She is a grandmother.
6. He is a father.

D. 1. She is my mother.
2. She is my sister.
3. He is my brother.
4. He is my grandfather.
5. She is my teacher.
6. He is my father.

Unit 3
My Body

What is it?, Plurals, What are they?

Vocabulary: arm, ear, eye, feet, foot, hand, leg, mouth, nose

Lesson Objectives

✓ to name body parts

✓ to ask and answer *What is it? It is a (mouth).*

Classroom English
- Find. Say. Color. Draw. Read. Show me. What is it? It is a (hand). It is an (eye). Touch your (nose).

Language Patterns
- What is it? It is a (hand). It is an (ear).

Materials
- crayons
- **Picture Cards:** arm, ear, eye, feet, foot, hand, leg, mouth, nose

WARMING UP

Say and model the following chant for students:

Touch your ear, touch your eye.
Touch your arm, touch your nose.
Touch your foot, touch your hand.
Touch your leg, touch your toes.

Say the chant slowly as you point to each body part. Encourage students to point to each body part as you say it in the chant. Now ask students to sit in a circle. Show students the Picture Cards. Hold up one card and model the vocabulary word. Ask students to repeat. Continue until all the vocabulary has been practiced. Ask: *What is it?* Model the response: *It is a (mouth).* Students practice answering the question as you hold up a Picture Card.

USING PAGE 27

Help students find page 27 in their books. Ask students: *What do you see?* Point to key vocabulary words on the page and model the response: *I see a (nose).* Ask students to

repeat. Point to the children in the picture. Model: *He is a boy. She is a girl.* Ask students to repeat.

Point to each vocabulary word and the corresponding picture. Play the recording or read and ask students to repeat. Encourage students to point to the words and the pictures.

Point to the picture of the boy who is being traced. Point to the key vocabulary words and ask: *What is it?* Students answer: *It is a (mouth).* Give the following directions and model the activity:
Show me a red crayon.
Find a hand.
Draw a circle around a hand.
Continue with different colors for each body part. Allow students to circle the body parts of any children in the picture.

HAVING FUN!
Find It

Place the Picture Cards faceup on the table. Invite students to say the words with you. Now turn over the Picture Cards. Individual students find the pictures when you say: *Find a (leg).* Students keep the cards they find. The student with the most cards at the end of the game wins.

Ask and Answer

Invite two students to take the parts of a short conversation. Model each students' part and ask them to repeat. Students then ask and answer:
Student 1: *What is it?*
Student 2: *It is a (mouth).*
Invite other students to ask and answer, using the other Picture Cards for body parts.

Vocabulary: arm, ear, eye, foot, hand, leg, mouth, nose

Lesson Objectives
✓ to name body parts
✓ to ask and answer *What is it? It is a (nose)*.
✓ to write questions and answers about body parts: *What is it? It is a (nose)*.
✓ to draw pictures for key words

Classroom English
• Find. Say. Color. Show me. Read. Write. Draw. Touch your (nose).

Language Patterns
• What is it? It is a (hand). It is an (ear).
• It is my (hand).

Materials
• index cards, drawing paper, glue, scissors, crayons, old magazines
• **Picture Cards:** arm, ear, eye, foot, hand, leg, mouth, nose

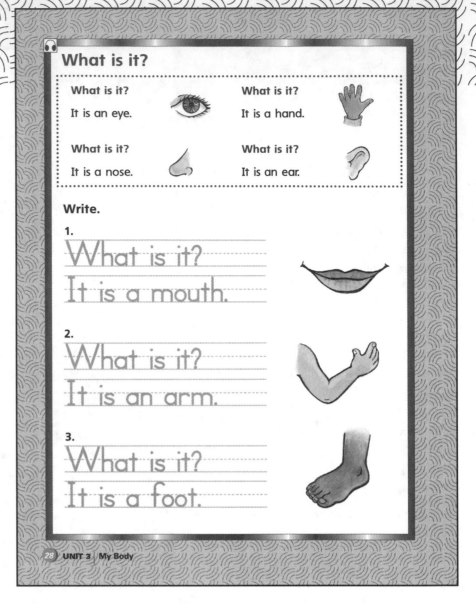

WARMING UP

Play a quick game of Simon Says. Say: *Simon says touch your (nose).* Students follow your directions and touch their (noses). If you do not say *Simon says,* students should not follow your directions. Use the unit vocabulary when playing.

Now show students the Picture Cards for this unit. Ask: *What is it?* Model the response: *It is a (nose).* Ask students to repeat. Practice all the unit vocabulary.

Write pairs of questions and answers on the board ahead of time for each body-part word. For example: *What is it? It is an eye. What is it? It is a hand.* Hold up the corresponding Picture Cards and read the questions and answers. Ask students to read with you. Practice reading each question and answer.

Show students how to write the questions and answers by tracing

them. Invite students to take turns tracing the questions and answers you have written on the board.

Remind students of the rule for using *a* for nouns that begin with a consonant sound and *an* for nouns that begin with a vowel sound.

USING PAGE 28

Help students find page 28 in their books. Ask them to tell what they see. Point to the pictures at the top of the page and ask: *What is it?* Model responses if necessary.

Play the recording or read the questions and answers aloud. Students listen to and then repeat the question and answer. Point to the corresponding pictures. Remind

students to point to each word as they read.

Allow each student to practice asking and answering the question. Invite two students to model the conversation. The first student asks the question and the second student answers it.

Point to the directions for the next activity and read with students. Point to the picture of the mouth and ask students to identify it. Read the question and answer with students and ask them to repeat. Show them how to complete the page by tracing the question and answer.

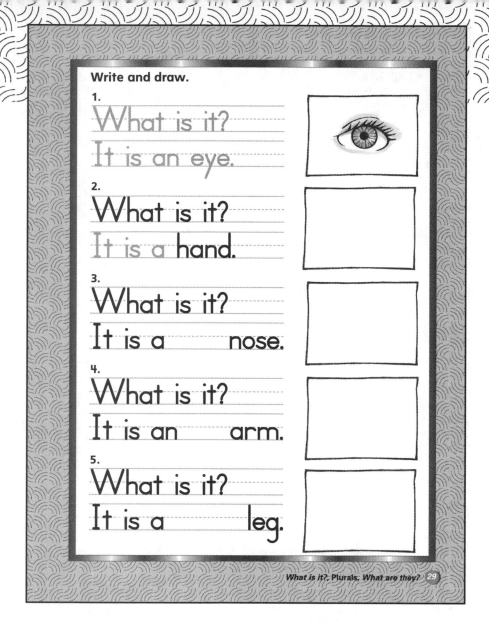

Write and draw.

1. What is it?
   It is an eye.

2. What is it?
   It is a hand.

3. What is it?
   It is a   nose.

4. What is it?
   It is an   arm.

5. What is it?
   It is a   leg.

What is it?, Plurals, What are they? 29

USING PAGE 29

Help students find page 29 in their books. Ask them to identify the body part on the page. Ask: *What is it?* as you point to the picture. Model the response if necessary: *It is an (eye).* Read the question and answer for number 1 and ask students to read with you.

Point to number 2. Read the words with students. Demonstrate how to draw a hand in the box. Model how to write the question on the line and ask students to do the same. Show students how to complete the response on the next line. Complete the page with students.

HAVING FUN!
Matching

Use the Picture Cards for this unit. Write the following words on index cards ahead of time: *arm, ear, eye, foot, hand, leg, mouth, nose.* Hold up the Picture Cards and the word cards. Read the words with students. Place the Picture Cards faceup on the floor or on a table in front of students. Place the word cards in a pile. Model the activity for students. Students come up, choose a word card, read it, and place it on the corresponding Picture Card.

Drawing Dictation

Show students how to fold their drawing paper into eight boxes. Help

them number the boxes 1–8. Give the following directions and ask students to draw with you: *Draw an eye.* Continue with *ear, nose, mouth, foot, leg, hand, arm.*

After students are finished drawing, model and play a Show Me game. Students point to and name the picture they have drawn when you say: *Show me a (foot).* Continue playing until everyone has had a turn. More advanced students can write the words under the pictures.

What is it?

Hold a body part Picture Card behind your back. Model the activity. Ask: *What is it?* Students take turns guessing: *It is a (leg).* The student who guesses correctly first gets to hold the next picture card behind his or her back while the rest of the class guesses.

Act It Out: *My*

Model the activity for students. Point to your (nose). Ask: *What is it?* Say: *It is my (nose).* Motion for students to point to their (noses) and repeat. Continue with the key vocabulary: *arm, ear, eye, foot, hand, leg, mouth, nose.*

Body Part Collages

Show students a finished collage. Point to body-part pictures you have cut out and ask students to identify them. Model the activity. Students cut out pictures of body parts from old magazines and make a collage by pasting them on drawing paper. When finished, ask students to sit in a circle. Model this short conversation and show students how to point to one of their pictures when they are asking the question:
Student 1: *What is it?*
Student 2: *It is a (nose).*

Vocabulary: arm, ear, eye, feet, foot, hand, leg, mouth, nose

Lesson Objectives
✓ to identify singular and plural body part names
✓ to use a final *s* at the end of plural words
✓ to use the irregular plural form *feet*

Classroom English
• Say. Write. Draw. Read. What is it? It is a (hand). It is an (ear). What are they? They are (hands).

Language Patterns
• What is it? It is a (hand).
• What are they? They are (arms).

Materials
• crayons
• **Picture Cards:** arm, ear, eye, foot, feet, hand, leg, mouth, nose

WARMING UP

Review singular body parts using Picture Cards. Ask: *What is it?* Students respond: *It is a (nose).*

Using the body-parts Picture Cards, model pronunciation for students, emphasizing the final *s* sound for the plurals. Now say the words in singular and plural pairs as you hold up the corresponding Picture Cards. Ask students to repeat. Tell students that when we have more than one of something we add the ending sound /z/.

Write the singular forms for the body-part words on the board. Read each word with students as you hold up the singular Picture Card. Now hold up the plural Picture Card for the first word and model the plural word. Students repeat. Write the plural form next to the singular form and underline the final *s* for each word. Draw pictures of arms, ears, eyes, hands, and legs. Read with students.

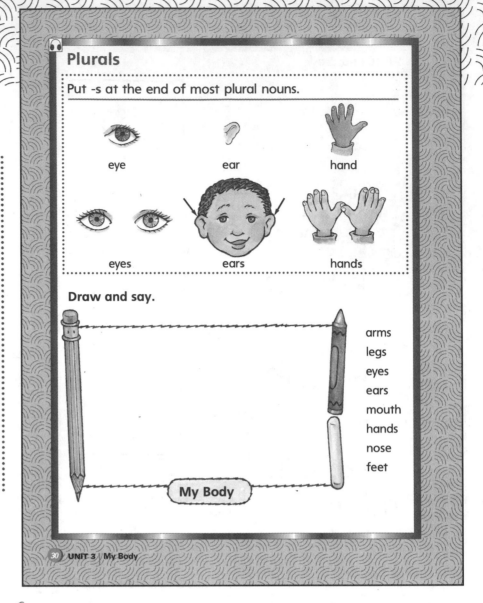

Plurals

Put -s at the end of most plural nouns.

eye ear hand

eyes ears hands

Draw and say.

arms
legs
eyes
ears
mouth
hands
nose
feet

My Body

UNIT 3 My Body

Tell students that when we have more than one of something, we add the letter *s* to the end of the word (noun). Save the irregular plural *feet* for last and tell students that this one is different. Model and ask students to repeat: *foot, feet.*

USING PAGE 30

Help students find page 30 in their books. Play the recording or read the Grammar Box and point to the pictures. Students should point to each pair of words with you. Tell students that when we have more than one of something we usually write the letter *-s* and say its sound at the end of the word.

Show students a picture of yourself that you have drawn ahead of time. Ask them to identify the body parts in your picture. Read the word list and ask students to read with you. Read the words *My Body.* Tell students to draw themselves. When they are finished, ask students to sit in a circle and talk about their pictures. Model first by holding up your picture and saying: *It is my (hand).*

HAVING FUN!
Listening Game

Say singular and plural body-part words. Students point to the body part(s) you name. For example: *leg,* students point to one leg; *legs,* students point to both legs.

Vocabulary: arm, arms, ear, ears, eye, eyes, hand, hands, leg, legs, foot, feet

Lesson Objectives

✓ to say and write the plural forms of nouns by adding *s*

✓ to ask and write the question *What are they?* for plural nouns

✓ to say and write the irregular plural *foot/feet*

Classroom English

• Draw. Say. Write. Show me. Close your eyes. Find.

Language Patterns

• What are they? They are (hands).

• What is it? It is a (hand). It is an (ear).

Materials

• crayons; pencils; drawing paper; index cards with the words: arm, ear, eye, foot, hand, leg, arms, ears, eyes, feet, hands, legs; pictures of the following body parts drawn on paper: two eyes, two ears, two arms, two feet, two hands, two legs, 1 mouth, 1 nose

• **Picture Cards:** arm, ear, eye, hand, leg, foot, feet

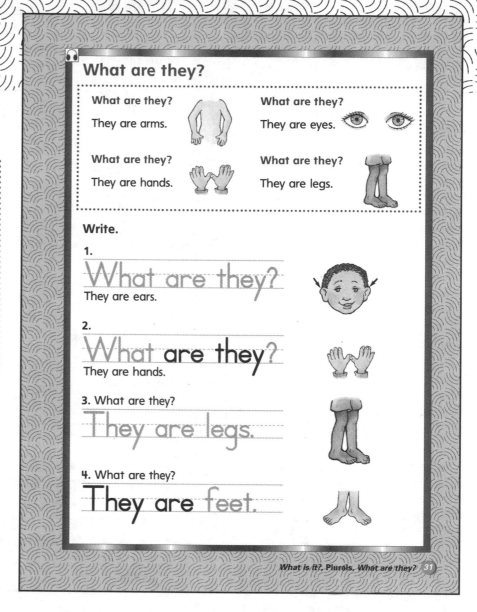

WARMING UP

Review the singular body-part words with students. Hold up a Picture Card and ask: *What is it?* Students respond: *It is a (hand).* Write the question and response on the board. Read with students. Invite students to trace the words in each sentence.

Point to the plural body parts on pages 31 and 32 and ask: *What are they?* Model the response: *They are (hands).* Ask the question for each plural Picture Card and model the responses. Students repeat. Write the questions and answers on the board. Read with students. Invite students to trace the words in the sentences.

Practice the questions and responses for singular and plural body parts. Write the questions and responses on

the board and ask students to read with you. Then invite individual students to come up and write the questions by tracing the words.

Write the following incomplete sentences on the board ahead of time and place the corresponding Picture Card next to it:

What _____ they?

_____ are legs.

What _____ it?

_____ is a mouth.

Point to the picture and ask the question. Point to the incomplete sentence and help students fill in the missing word. Tell them that we use the words *they* and *are* for plural nouns and the words *it* and *is* for singular nouns.

USING PAGE 31

Help students find page 31 in their books. Ask them to identify the body parts on the page. Play the recording or read the questions and answers. Ask students to repeat. Tell them that we use the question and response: *What are they? They are (hands).* for plural nouns. Read the directions for the next activity and ask students to read with you. Point to the body part for each example and ask students to tell what they see. Read the question and answer and ask them to read with you. Show students how to write the question by tracing the words. Complete the page with the class.

USING PAGE 32

Help students find page 32 in their books. Ask them to identify the body parts on the page. Read the example. Remind students that we use *they* and *are* for plural questions and responses. Help students find the picture of the *legs* and show them how to draw a line to match the sentence to the picture. Continue with the other sentences. Remind students when to use singular and plural forms. Complete the page with students.

HAVING FUN!
Memory Game: Find the Pair

Write the following words on one set of index cards: *arm, ear, eye, foot, hand, leg.* Write the plural forms on another set of index cards: *arms, ears, eyes, feet, hands, legs.* Read each set of words with students. Place them facedown on a table or on the floor in front of students. Students take turns turning over two cards. If they find the singular and plural, they keep the pair. The student with the most pairs at the end of the game wins. Encourage students to read the words and point to the corresponding body part(s) as they are playing.

Draw and Ask

Model the activity. Tell students to draw the body part(s) of their choice on a piece of drawing paper. Then ask them to sit in a circle. Model the activity. Turn to the student on your right and ask: *What is it?* or *What are they?* depending on the picture they drew. Students tell what they have drawn: *It is a (hand).* or *They are (feet).* Continue around the circle until each student has had a turn to ask and answer about the pictures.

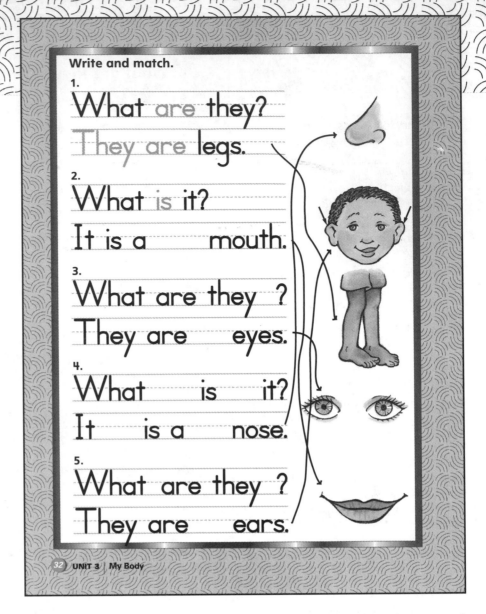

Close Your Eyes

Draw the outline of a large clown on the board. Draw each of the following body parts on drawing paper for students to put on the clown: two eyes, two ears, two arms, two feet, two hands, two legs, one mouth, one nose. Place a piece of double-sided tape on the back of each picture. Before playing, ask students to identify the body parts as you ask: *What is it?* or *What are they?*

Model the activity. Invite a student to come up and give him or her a picture of a body part. Ask the student to identify the body part after you ask the appropriate question. Now ask the student to close his or her eyes and to walk to the clown.

The student then places the picture of the body part where he or she thinks it belongs. Continue until all the pictures have been placed. When the picture is complete, fix any mistakes to make the picture correct.

Vocabulary: arm, arms, ear, ears, eye, eyes, foot, feet, hand, hands, leg, legs, mouth, nose

Lesson Objectives
✓ to say a chant about body parts
✓ to identify body parts, singular and plural
✓ to ask and answer questions for singular and plural nouns
✓ to follow directions and color

Classroom English
• Color. Show me. Find. Say. What is it? It is a (hand). It is an (ear). What are they? They are (hands).

Language Patterns
• What is it? It is a (mouth). It is an (ear).
• What are they? They are (ears).

Materials
• crayons
• **Picture Cards:** arm, ear, eye, foot, feet, hand, leg, mouth, nose

USING PAGE 33

Help students find page 33 in their books. Show the Picture Cards for this unit. Ask students to identify each one. Ask: *What is it?* or *What are they?* Help them respond: *It is a (nose).* or *They are (ears).*

Play the recording or read the chant aloud. Model and ask students to follow along and point to each word in the chant as they listen. After they have listened to and read the chant a few times, invite them to say it with you. Encourage them to point to each word as they read and then to find the corresponding picture.

Divide the class into two groups. Group 1 can ask the question and group 2 can say the response. Allow students to practice both parts.

🎧 **Chant.**

What is it?
It's a nose.
It's a nose.
It's a nose.

What is it?
It's a mouth.
It's a mouth.
It's a mouth.

What are they?
They're ears.
They're ears.
They're ears.

What are they?
They're hands.
They're hands.
They're hands.

They're = They are
It's = It is

What is it?, Plurals, *What are they?* 33

Tell them that we can change *They are* to *They're*. Tell students that we can change *It is* to *It's*. Show students that we omit the letter *i* and use an apostrophe for the word *it's* and omit the letter *a* and use an apostrophe for the word *they're*.

USING PAGE 34

Help students find page 34 in their books. Ask them to talk about the picture and play a Show Me game. Say sentences such as: *Show me a (hand). Show me (eyes).* Read the directions for them as they follow along. *Show me a red crayon. They are hands. Color the hands.*

Continue with different colors for the rest of the body parts. Complete the page with students. When finished, ask students to sit in a circle with their pictures. Students can ask and answer: *What is it? It is a (hand). What are they? They are (hands).*

EXTENSION
Continue the Chant

Review the chant with students by playing the recording or reading it aloud. Substitute other body-part words. Hold up a Picture Card as a prompt. Students say the chant for that picture.

Color.

34 UNIT 3 | My Body

Unit 4
Clothes

This/That, These/Those, Adjectives

Vocabulary: coat, dress, hat, pants, shirt, shoe, skirt, sock, sweater

Lesson Objectives

✓ to name clothing items

✓ to use singular demonstrative pronouns *this* and *that*

Classroom English

• Find. Say. Circle. Color. Draw. Listen. Write. Show me. What is this/that?

Language Patterns

• This is a (sock).

• That is a (shoe).

Materials

• a big paper bag

• **Realia:** dress, skirt, shirt, shoe, pants, sweater, coat, sock, hat

• **Picture Cards:** dress, skirt, shirt, shoe, pants, sweater, coat, sock, hat

WARMING UP

Show students the Picture Cards for clothing words or use real clothing if available: *dress, skirt, shirt, shoe, sweater, coat, sock, hat.* Model each word and ask them to repeat after you.

Present the vocabulary word *pants* last. Help students practice saying: *They are pants.* Tell them that this is a special word and does not use *It is.*

Pick up one of the Picture Cards and ask: *What is this?* Model the response: *This is a (dress).* Ask students to repeat. Practice each vocabulary word using the word *this.* Write the sentence: *This is a (dress).* on the board and ask students to read with you. Invite students to come up and trace each word in the sentence as they read for the rest of the class.

Now take the Picture Cards and place them far away from where you are. Point to one of the cards and ask: *What is that?* Emphasize the word

Clothes

UNIT 4

This/That, These/Those, **Adjectives** 35

that. Model the response: *That is a (dress).* Practice each vocabulary word using the word *that.*

Write the sentence: *That is a (dress).* on the board and ask students to read with you. Invite students to come up and trace each word in the sentence as they read for the rest of the class.

USING PAGE 35

Help students find page 35 in their books. Students identify what they see. Point to items of clothing and ask: *What is this?* Model responses if necessary. Point to each item and word. Play the recording or read each one for students. Students repeat. Play a Show Me game with students.

Say: *Show me a (sweater).* Students point to the *(sweater).* Continue practicing each word on the page.

Give directions and complete the page with students. Hold up a (red) crayon and say: *Find red. Circle the dress.* Continue with different colors for each of the new vocabulary words on the page.

USING PAGE 36

Help students find page 36 in their books. Play the recording or read the Grammar Box as you point to the pictures. Students read with you. Tell students that we use the word *this* when things are close to us and we use the word *that* when things are far away.

Now read the directions for the writing activity. Students follow along. Point to the picture of the girl. Point to her skirt and ask: *What is this?* Model the response and read: *This is a skirt.* Ask students to read with you and to point to each word in the sentence as they are reading. Now ask students to trace the words in this sentence. Complete the page with students. Students read and trace the words.

HAVING FUN!
Guessing Game

Play a guessing game. Bring in realia for these items: shoe, sock, hat, shirt. Place these items in a large bag so students can't see them. Model the activity. Invite students to come up and feel what is in the bag. After everyone has had a turn to feel the items, ask individual students to guess what the items are. As students guess, place the items on the floor. Model responses and ask them to repeat: *This is a (shoe).*

Show Me

Use the Picture Cards for *coat, shirt, skirt, dress, sweater,* and *hat.* Place some on the floor in front of you. Place some in different parts of the room so they are far away. Say: *That is a (dress). Show me.* or *This is a (skirt). Show me.* Students point to the Picture Card.

Find This and That

Use real clothing for this activity. You will need two of each clothing item.

Practice these words: *coat, shirt, skirt, dress, sweater, sock, hat.* Place one Picture Card near where you and the students are sitting and place another in a different part of the room so that it is far away. Model the activity. Say: *Find this (sweater). Find that (sweater).* Choose a student. He or she points to the item that is close and says: *This is a (sweater).* Then the student finds the (sweater) that is far away and says: *That is a (sweater).*

Listen and Stand

Model the activity. Say a clothing word. If students are wearing the clothing word you name, they stand, point to what they are wearing, and say: *This is a (skirt).* If they are not wearing what you say, they remain seated.

What's Missing?

Place the clothing Picture Cards on the floor or on a table in front of students. Point to each one and ask: *What is this?* Students point to the picture and respond: *This is a (skirt).* Ask them to close their eyes. Take away one card. Ask students to open their eyes. Point to the place where the card is missing and invite them to guess what card you took away. The student who guesses correctly first gets to take away the next card.

Vocabulary: dress, sweater, shoes, socks, skirt, hats, pants, coats, shirts

Lesson Objectives
✓ to identify singular and plural clothing items
✓ to use singular and plural demonstrative pronouns *this, that, these,* and *those*

Classroom English
• Say. Write. Find. Show me. What is this/that? What are these/those?

Language Patterns
• This is a (skirt).
• That is a (shoe).
• These are (skirts).
• Those are (pants).

Materials
• drawing paper and crayons, bingo grids with nine spaces (one for each student), bingo markers
• **Realia:** dress, sweater, shoes, socks, skirts, hats, pants, coats, shirts
• **Picture Cards:** dress, sweater, shoe, sock, skirt, hat, coat, shirt, pants

These/Those

These are shoes.   Those are shoes.

These are socks.   Those are socks.

Write.
1. These are pants.
2. Those are hats.
3. These are coats.
4. Those are shirts.

This/That, These/Those, Adjectives 37

WARMING UP

Ask students to sit in a circle. Place the Picture Cards or clothing items close enough for students to touch. Point to the *(shoe).* Ask: *What is this?* Model the response and ask students to repeat: *This is a (shoe).* Point to real *shoes* and ask: *What are these?* Model the response and ask them to repeat: *These are (shoes).* Practice these pairs of words. Use *this* and *these* and clothing words. Write examples on the board: *This is a (skirt). These are (skirts).* Read with students and invite them to come up and trace the sentences.

Place a *hat* in one corner of the room. Place two *hats* in a different part of the room. Point to the *hat* and ask: *What is that?* Model the response and ask students to repeat:

That is a hat. Point to the hats and ask: *What are those?* Model the response and ask students to repeat: *Those are hats.* Place other singular and plural clothes far away from where the students are sitting. Practice *these* and *those* with clothing words. Write example sentences on the board. Read them with students and invite them to come up and trace the sentences.

On the board, write: *This/That is a hat.* Place the hat Picture Card far from you and ask: *What is that?* Read the example and help students see *that* best finishes the sentence. Circle the word *that.* Provide additional examples for singular and plural clothing words using *this, that, these, those.* Read the sentences with students and ask them

to circle the word that best completes the sentence.

Remind students that we use the word *this* for singular words that are close to us. We use the word *that* for singular words that are far away.

USING PAGE 37

Help students find page 37 in their books. Play the recording or read the Grammar Box with students. Ask them to follow along. Point to the pictures as you read. Tell students that we use *these* for plural items that are close to us. We use *those* for plural items that are far away.

Read the directions for the writing activity with students. Point to the first picture and ask them to tell what they see. Read the sentences with students. Tell students to identify the clothing item and then to read and trace the sentence.

USING PAGE 38

Help students find page 38 in their books. Read the directions with them. Point to the picture in number 1. Ask: *What is this?* as you point to the girl's dress. Model the response: *This is a dress.* Point to each word as you read. Point to number 2 and ask: *What is that?* Model the response: *That is a sweater.* Help students find and circle the word *that* and read the completed sentence. Complete the page with students.

HAVING FUN!
Identify what You Are Wearing

Model the activity. Point to what you are wearing and say: *This is a (sweater). These are (shoes).* Ask students to sit in a circle. Students take turns identifying what they are wearing using *this* and *these*.

Draw

Give each student a piece of drawing paper and show them how to fold it into eight spaces. Show them how to number the spaces 1–8. Model the activity. Say: *1. Draw a hat.* Continue with seven different singular and plural items. (Students' answers will vary in number for the plural pictures.) When students are finished drawing, invite them to sit in a circle. Hold up your paper and point to one of your pictures. Say: *This is a (sock).* Turn to the student on your right. Point to one of their pictures. Model the correct response if necessary and ask them to repeat. Continue until everyone has had a chance to participate.

Memory Game

Place the clothing Picture Cards on the floor or on a table in front of

Look and circle.

1. (This)/ That is a dress.

2. This /(That) is a sweater.

3. These /(Those) are shoes.

4. (These)/ Those are socks.

5. (This)/ These is a skirt.

6. That /(Those) are hats.

students. Point to each one and ask: *What is this? What are these?* Students point to the Picture Card and respond: *This is a (sweater). These are (shoes).* Now turn over the Picture Cards so students can't see them. Say: *Find the (shoes).* Students take turns turning over one card. If they find the correct picture, they keep the card and say: *This is a (shoe).* The student with the most cards at the end of the game wins.

Clothing Bingo

Prepare bingo grids with nine spaces for each student. Use paper clips or small pieces of paper for markers. Give each student a grid. Tell students that everyone's bingo grid should be different, and to draw their pictures in

any space on the paper. Give directions: *Draw a (dress).* Continue with directions for: *shoes, socks, shirts, skirt, pants, socks, hat, hats.* Call out a word. Students place markers on the pictures. Three in a row wins. The winner says a sentence for each word in the winning row: *This is a (sock). These are (hats).*

Vocabulary: big, black, blue, brown, coat, dress, green, hat, long, orange, pants, red, shirt, shoes, short, skirt, small, sweater, white, yellow,

Lesson Objectives
✓ to name clothing items
✓ to use adjectives
✓ to use demonstrative pronouns *this, that, these, those*

Classroom English
• Draw. Show me. Find. Listen. Say. What is this/that? What are these/those?

Language Patterns
• This is a (shoe). That is a (shoe).
• These are (shoes). Those are (shoes).
• This is a (big)(shoe). That is a (big)(shoe).
• These are (red)(shoes). Those are (red)(shoes).

Materials
• color cards, old magazines, glue, scissors
• **Realia:** pants, skirt, dress, shoes, hat, sweater, coat, shirt
• **Picture Cards:** pants, skirt, dress, shoes, hat, sweater, coat, shirt

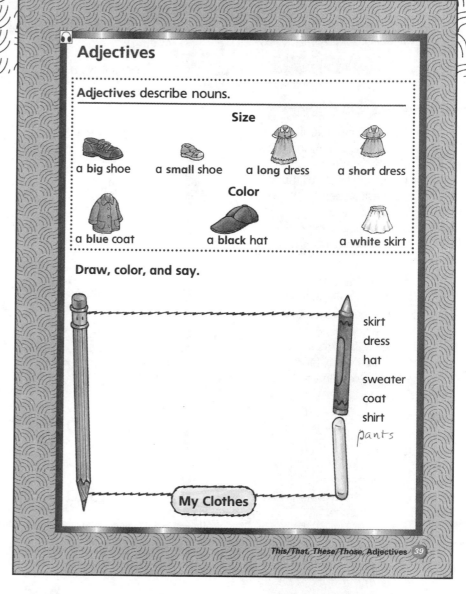

Adjectives

Adjectives describe nouns.

Size

a big shoe | a small shoe | a long dress | a short dress

Color

a blue coat | a black hat | a white skirt

Draw, color, and say.

skirt
dress
hat
sweater
coat
shirt
pants

My Clothes

This/That, These/Those, Adjectives 39

WARMING UP

Draw these pairs of pictures on the board ahead of time or use real clothing if available:

a long dress	a short dress
a long sweater	a short sweater
a big shirt	a small shirt
a big shoe	a small shoe

Ask students to tell what they see. Ask students to repeat: *This is a (long) (dress).* as you point to each picture.

Review color words with students. Hold up one of the clothing Picture Cards and model: *a (blue) (coat). This is a (blue) (coat).* Ask students to repeat. Review the other color

words and pair them with clothing words. Write examples on the board for students to read.

USING PAGE 39

Help students find page 39 in their books. Students tell what they see. Play the recording or read the Grammar Box for students as they follow along. Point to each picture as you read. Ask students to read chorally. Tell students that the words *big, small, long,* and *short* talk about size.

For the next activity, show students a picture of what you are wearing, that you have drawn and colored ahead of time. Point to each clothing item in your picture and model responses: *a*

(red)(shirt). Read the directions and ask students to follow along. Point to each word and ask students to point and read with you. Students draw what they are wearing or their favorite outfit. When they are finished, students point to, name, and describe the clothing items they have drawn.

USING PAGE 40

Help students find page 40 in their books. Ask students to tell what they see. Point to the picture in number 1 and ask: *What is this?* Model the response and ask students to repeat: *This is a big dress.* Read both sentences with students. Help them see that the first sentence goes with the picture.

Point to number 2 and ask students to tell what they see. Read the sentences with them. Help students see that the second sentence goes with the picture. Show them how to place a check in the box for this sentence. Complete number 3 with students.

Read the directions for the next activity and ask students to read with you. Point to the picture in number 1 and ask students to tell what they see. Read the sentence and tell students to trace the words to complete the sentence.

Point to number 2 and ask students to tell what they see. Read, trace the words, and complete the sentence with students: *This is a red shoe.* Complete the rest of the page with students by filling in the missing words.

HAVING FUN!
Show Me Colors and Size

Model the activity. Say: *Show me (red).* Students point to something red in the classroom. If it is a word they have practiced, allow them to name it and describe it by using a color word: *a red pencil.* Practice the color words: *red, yellow, blue, green, brown, black, white, orange.*

Repeat this activity using size words: *big, small, long, short.*

I Spy

Use classroom object words from Unit 1 that students are familiar with and

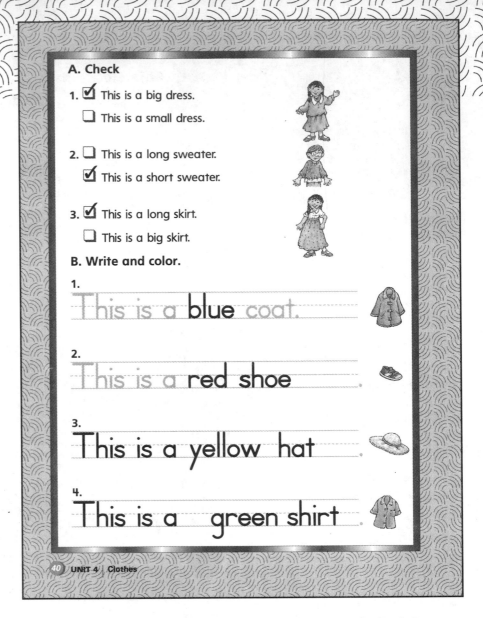

clothing words from this unit. Students listen to clues you give them about an item in the classroom. For example: *Small. Yellow.* Students look around and try to find the object. The student who guesses first tells what it is and describes it: *(This/That) is a small pencil. (This/That) is a yellow pencil.*

Dress-Up Race

Bring in large, old clothes for students to play dress-up. Choose two students to play. Make a pile of clothes for each student ahead of time. Try to make the task equal for each student by placing similar clothing in each pile. Say: *Go!* Students get dressed as fast as they can. They must tie shoes, zipper, and button all clothing to be the winner.

When they are finished, ask them to describe what they are wearing. For example: *This is a (big) (shirt).*

Clothing Collages

Show students a collage you have prepared ahead of time. Point to the pictures and describe them using color and size words: *This is a (long) (coat).* Students cut out pictures from old magazines to make their collages. When they are finished, ask them to sit in a circle. Invite individual students to come up, point to the pictures in their collages, and describe them using color and size words. Prompt them by pointing to one of their pictures and asking: *What is this? What are these?*

Vocabulary: big, black, blue, brown, coat, dress, green, hat, long, orange, pants, red, shirt, shoes, short, skirt, small, sweater, white, yellow

Lesson Objectives
✓ to name clothing items
✓ to use adjectives
✓ to use singular and plural demonstrative pronouns: *this, that, these, those*

Classroom English
• Say. Show me. Find. Listen. Go to. What is this/that? What are these/those?

Language Patterns
• This is a (big) (shirt). That is a (big) (shirt).
• These are (red) (shoes). Those are (red) (shoes).

Materials
• crayons, a string to make a clothes-line, colored construction paper
• **Realia:** dress, sweater, skirt, coat, hat, shoes, pants
• **Picture Cards:** dress, sweater, skirt, coat, hat, shoes, shirt, pants

🎧 **Chant.**

What's this?
It's a sweater.
What's that?
It's a dress.

What's this?
It's a shirt.
What's that?
It's a hat.

What are those?
They're socks.
What are those?
They're shoes.

what's = what is
it's = it is
they're = they are

This/That, These/Those, Adjectives ④①

USING PAGE 41

Help students find page 41 in their books. Place the following Picture Cards far away from you: *dress, hat, socks, shoes.* Hold the following Picture Cards in your hand: *sweater, shirt.* Act out the chant by holding or pointing to the appropriate Picture Card as you say the chant. Play the recording or read the chant for students. Model and ask them to follow along and point to each word as they listen. After students have listened to and read the chant a few times, invite them to say it with you. Encourage them to point to each word as they read and then to find the corresponding picture to each stanza.

Divide the class into two groups. Group 1 asks the question and group 2 tells the response. Allow students to practice both parts.

EXTENSION
Continue the Chant

Review the chant with students by playing the recording or reading it for them. Substitute other clothing words. Hold up a Picture Card as a prompt.

USING PAGE 42

Show Me

Help students find page 42 in their books. Play a Show Me game with them. Say sentences such as: *Show me a sock.* Now read the directions as students follow along. Point to the children at the bottom of the page. Ask: *Who is it?* Model responses if necessary. Show students how to draw a line from the child to his or her clothing. Complete the page. When students are finished, ask them to color the clothing.

EXTENSION

Talk about the Picture

Model sentences using size and color words: *This is a (red) (sock). These are (green) (shoes).* Ask students to say additional sentences about the picture. Prompt them by pointing to the pictures they have colored.

Make a Clothes Line

Ask students to draw a picture of a piece of clothing: *pants, shirt, skirt, sweater, coat,* or *hat* on a piece of colored construction paper. Students then cut out the pictures. Hang these pictures on a clothes line made of string. Provide time at the beginning or end of class for students to talk about the pictures they have drawn. Encourage them to use size and color words to describe the pictures.

Match and color.

42 UNIT 4 | Clothes

Units 3 & 4
Review

Vocabulary: skirt, coat, hat, sweater, sock(s), pants, dress, shirt(s), eye(s), mouth, leg(s), hand(s), foot (feet), ear(s), arm(s)

Review Objectives
✓ to name clothing items

✓ to name body parts

✓ to use singular and plural nouns

✓ to use descriptive adjectives

✓ to use demonstrative pronouns *this, that, these, those*

Classroom English
• Listen. Check. Color. Point. Say.

• (This/That) is a (coat). (These/Those) are (eyes).

Language Patterns
• This is a (coat). That is a (coat).

• These are (pants). Those are (pants).

Materials
• crayons

• **Realia:** skirt, coat, hat, sweater, socks, pants, dress, shirts

• **Picture Cards:** skirt, coat, hat, sweater, sock, pants, dress, shirt, eye, mouth, leg, hand, foot, ear, arm

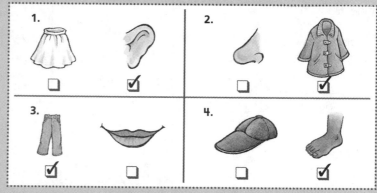

Review: Units 3 and 4

Vocabulary
🎧 **A. Listen and check.**

Plurals
🎧 **B. Listen and check.**

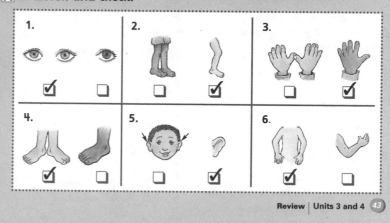

Review | Units 3 and 4 43

WARMING UP

Review the vocabulary words from Units 3 and 4 with students. Use the Picture Cards or realia. Ask: *What is it?* Invite students to use a complete sentence when answering: *It is a (sock).*

After students have practiced saying the singular and plural nouns in isolation, model sentences for them: *This is a (shirt). These are (shirts).* Hold up singular and plural Picture Cards and invite students to say sentences using the correct form.

Review the demonstrative pronouns *this* and *that* with students. Place one Picture Card close to you and say: *This is a (sweater).* Place a second card far away from you and say: *That is a (dress).* Ask students to say these with you. Now place different Picture Cards close and far away. Invite students to say sentences using *this* and *that.* Model if necessary.

If you feel students need to practice exercises that are similar to those presented in the Review Units, use exercises similar to the ones described for Review Units 1 and 2, pages 25–26. Students can practice checking boxes and pictures that go with sentences and words that are said.

AUDIOSCRIPT

A. 1. ear   2. coat   3. pants   4. foot

B. 1. eyes   2. leg   3. hand   4. feet   5. ear   6. arms

USING PAGE 43

Help students find page 43 in their books. Help students find Exercise A. Read the directions and ask them to follow along. Point to each picture and ask students to say the words with you. Explain that they should listen and check the picture that goes with the word that they hear. Play the recording or read the audioscript for students. Students check the correct picture.

Help students find Exercise B. Read the directions and ask them to follow along. Point to the pictures and ask students to repeat each word after you. Explain that students should check the box that goes with the word. Play the recording or read the audioscript. Students should check the picture that goes with the - sentence that they hear.

USING PAGE 44

Help students find page 44 in their books. Help students find Exercise C. Read the directions and ask them to follow along. Explain to students that they should listen and color the pictures. Play the recording or read the audioscript for students. Students color the pictures according to the directions.

Help students find Exercise D. Read the directions and ask them to follow along. Explain that they should listen, point to the picture, and then say the word. Play the recording or read the audioscript for students.

Adjectives
🎧 C. Listen and color.

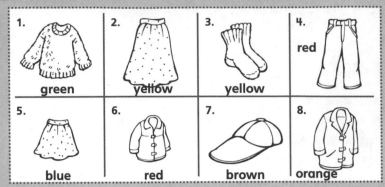

This/That, These/Those
🎧 D. Listen, point, and say.

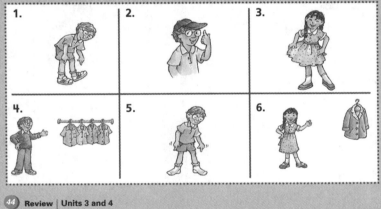

AUDIOSCRIPT

C. 1. Color the sweater green. 2. Color the long skirt yellow. 3. Color the socks yellow. 4. Color the pants red.
5. Color the short skirt blue. 6. Color the small coat red. 7. Color the hat brown. 8. Color the big coat orange.

D. 1. These are shoes. 2. This is a hat. 3. This is a dress. 4. Those are shirts.
5. These are socks. 6. That is a coat.

Unit 5
My House

Prepositions, *Where ...?*, Present Progressive

Vocabulary: bathroom, bed, bedroom, box, chair, clock, in, kitchen, lamp, living room, on, picture, table, tub, under

Lesson Objectives
✓ to name household items
✓ to name rooms in a house

Classroom English
• Find. Say. Circle. Color. Put. Draw. Listen. Write. Show me. What is this? What is it? Where is the (clock)?

Language Patterns
• What is this? This is a (bedroom).
• It is a (kitchen).
• The (clock) is (under) the (table).

Materials
• crayons, drawing paper
• **Realia:** big box, clock, table, chair, picture
• **Picture Cards:** lamp, chair, table, picture, box, tub, bed, clock, kitchen, living room, bedroom, bathroom

My House

box
bedroom
clock
lamp
kitchen
bed
tub
bathroom
picture
living room
chair
table

Prepositions, *Where ...?*, Present Progressive **45**

WARMING UP

Show students the Picture Cards for the following words or use realia: *box, tub, bed, clock, table, chair, lamp, bathroom, bedroom, living room, kitchen.* As you hold up each Picture Card or item, model the new word and ask students to repeat. After students are comfortable with the new words, ask: *What is this?* Model the response: *This is a (clock).* Students practice asking and answering the question using the new vocabulary words.

Ask students to close their eyes. Place the clock or the Picture Card for the clock in the box. Ask: *Where is the clock?* and shrug your shoulders. Allow students to answer with gestures or vocabulary they are comfortable with. Show them the

clock in the box and model the response: *In the box.* Ask students to repeat just the prepositional phrase at first. When they are familiar with this, ask them to repeat: *The clock is in the box.* Place other realia or Picture Cards in the box and ask students to tell where they are.

Introduce the prepositions *under* and *on* in the same way. Ask students to first repeat the prepositional phrases *on the (box)* and *under the (box)*. Then ask them to repeat the complete response: *The (clock) is (under) the (box).*

USING PAGE 45

Help students find page 45 in their books. Students identify what they

see. Point to items in the picture and ask: *What is this?* Model responses if necessary. Play the recording or read each word. Point to each item. Students repeat. Play a Show Me game. Say: *Show me a (bed).* Students point to the (bed). Continue practicing each word on the page.

Give the following directions and complete the page with students:
Draw a yellow circle around the clock.
Draw an orange circle around the tub.
Continue with different colors for each of the vocabulary words.

USING PAGE 46

Help students find page 46 in their books. Play the recording or read the Grammar Box as you point to the pictures. Students read with you. Tell students that these words show where things are. Now read the directions for the writing activity. Students follow along. Point to each picture. Ask students to tell what they see and to tell where the lamp, clock, and picture are. Read number 1 with them. Help students see that this sentence goes with the last picture. Ask them to draw the line. Ask them to trace the preposition. Complete the page with students.

HAVING FUN!
Put the (clock) in the box.

Use realia or Picture Cards from this unit. Model the activity. Give directions such as: *The (clock) is (under) the box. Put the clock under the box.* Invite students to come up and place the Picture Card or item in the correct place. Then invite them to tell where it is. Model responses if necessary.

Go to the (bedroom).

Model the activity. Place the room Picture Cards in different corners of the classroom. Point to them and ask: *What is that?* Help students respond: *That is the (kitchen).* After they have practiced the vocabulary, give directions: *Go to the (kitchen).* Students go to that Picture Card.

Drawing Dictation

Give students a piece of drawing paper and show them how to fold it into eight boxes. Give students crayons to draw and color with. Show them how to number the boxes from 1–8. Give the following directions:

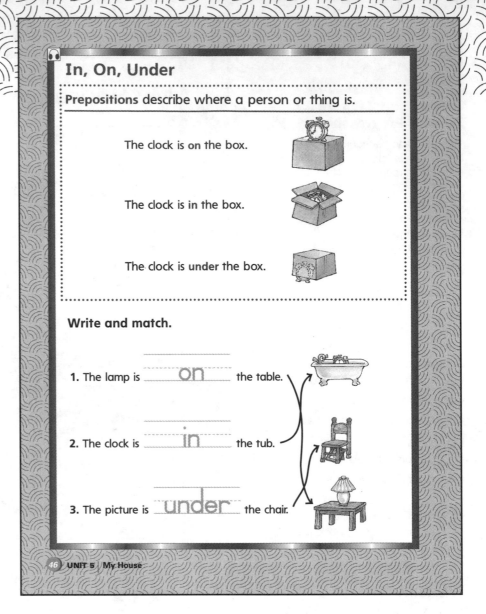

In, On, Under

Prepositions describe where a person or thing is.

The clock is on the box.

The clock is in the box.

The clock is under the box.

Write and match.

1. The lamp is ___on___ the table.

2. The clock is ___in___ the tub.

3. The picture is ___under___ the chair.

46 UNIT 5 My House

1. *Draw a red clock.*
2. *Draw a green tub.*
3. *Draw a blue bed.*
4. *Draw an orange lamp.*
5. *Draw a yellow table.*
6. *Draw a green chair.*
7. *Draw a red picture.*
8. *Draw a blue box.*

More advanced students can draw pictures that use prepositions:

1. *Draw a clock on a bed.,* etc.

Where is the (clock)?

Use the Picture Cards for: *chair, table, picture, tub, bed, clock.* Ahead of time, place the Picture Cards around the room, placing them in, on, and under familiar items. Ask students to find each item. Students can work in teams. Give one direction at a time: *Find the clock.* Students hunt in the classroom to find the Picture Card. The student or team who finds it first wins a point and tells where the item is: *The (clock) is (under) the (chair).* The student or team with the most points at the end of the game wins.

Vocabulary: bed, box, clock, in, it, lamp, on, picture, table, tub, under

Lesson Objectives

✓ to name household items

✓ to name rooms in the house

✓ to use *where*

✓ to use prepositions

✓ to use the subject pronoun *it*

Classroom English

• Say. Write. Find. Show me. Where is the (lamp)? What is this?

Language Patterns

• Where is the (lamp)? The (lamp) is (in) the (box).

• What is this? It is a (lamp).

• This is a (clock).

Materials

• big box, drawing paper, crayons, index cards with: *in, on, under*

• **Realia:** clock, table, chair, picture, lamp

• **Picture Cards:** lamp, clock, table, box, tub, picture, bed

Where ...?

Where is the clock?
It is on the table.

Where is the lamp?
It is in the box.

Write and match.

1. Where is the clock?
It is in the tub.

2. Where is the picture?
It is under the table.

3. Where is the lamp?
It is on the bed.

Prepositions, *Where ...?*, Present Progressive 47

WARMING UP

Ask students to sit in a circle. Use realia or Picture Cards. Place the (lamp) (in) the box and ask: *Where is the (lamp)?* Help students respond: *The (lamp) is (in) the box.* Students repeat. Continue practicing by putting other household items in, on, and under the box. Write the following questions and answers on the board ahead of time and draw a simple picture to illustrate each sentence: *Where is the clock? It is in the box. Where is the lamp? It is on the table. Where is the picture? It is under the table.*

Read the questions and answers with students. Help them see that the noun is replaced by the subject pronoun *it.* Invite students to come up, read, and trace the questions and answers.

USING PAGE 47

Help students find page 47 in their books. Play the recording or read the Grammar Box with students. Ask them to follow along and read with you. Point to the pictures as you read. Tell students that we use the question word *where* when we want to find something or someone. Read the directions for the writing activity with students. Point to each picture. Students tell what they see and where the items are. Read number 1 with them. Show students how to draw a line from the sentence to the matching picture. Now ask students to trace and write the missing words in each question and answer. Complete the page with students. Ask them to identify the pictures and then read and trace the sentences.

USING PAGE 48

Help students find page 48 in their books. Read the directions for Exercise A with them. Point to the picture in number 1. Ask: *What is this?* as you point to the chair and the lamp. Now ask: *Where is the lamp?* Model the response: *The lamp is on the chair.* Now ask students to read the sentence in number 1 with you. Point to each word as you read. Help students see that the word *on* best finishes the sentence. Continue in this manner, having students first describe the pictures, then read and complete the sentences by circling the correct word. Read the directions for Exercise B with students. Ask them to tell what they see in the picture and to tell where the item is. Read each question with students. As you read, point to each word and ask students to read with you. Help students complete the sentences by filling in the missing word and tracing the remaining words in the responses. Model all responses for students by writing words on the board for them.

HAVING FUN!
My House

Show students a completed picture to use as a model. Fold a piece of drawing paper into four sections. Label the boxes: *kitchen, living room, bedroom, bathroom.* Show students how to write these words in the boxes to label the rooms in their houses. Give the following directions and complete a picture with them: *Find the bathroom. Draw a tub in the bathroom. Find the kitchen. Draw a table in the kitchen.* Continue with the other rooms and unit vocabulary. When students' pictures are finished, ask them to sit in a circle. Model talking about your picture. For example: *This is the bedroom. The bed is in the bedroom.* Invite students to come up and talk about their pictures. More advanced

A. Circle.

1. The lamp is in / (on) / under the chair.

2. The clock is in / on / (under) the box.

3. The clock is (in) / on / under the box.

4. The picture is in / (on) / under the table.

B. Write.

1. Where is the lamp?

It is **under** the table.

2. Where is the clock?

It is **on the bed**.

3. Where is the picture?

It is **in the box**.

students can draw additional items in their houses. Model the words for them if necessary when they are talking about their pictures.

In, On, Under

Use vocabulary from this unit. Write the following words on index cards ahead of time: *in, on, under.* Read each word with students. Now put objects in, on, or under a box. Ask students: *Where is the (clock)?* Model responses if necessary and ask students to repeat. After students have told where the object is, invite them to come up and find the preposition that tells where the item is. For students with limited English ability, place the word index cards in front of them. Point to each one and read them for students. Then ask

them to find the correct word. Students with more English ability can find the word independently.

Sorting

Place the following Picture Cards on the floor in front of students: bedroom, bathroom, kitchen, living room. Ask: *What is this?* Now show students these Picture Cards, one at a time: *lamp, chair, table, picture, box, tub, bed, clock.* Ask students to tell what they see. Invite students to come up and place the Picture Cards on top of the room picture where they think each one belongs. Encourage students to tell where each item is: *The lamp is in the bedroom.* Answers will vary.

Vocabulary: eating, reading, sleeping, watching

WARMING UP

Show students a picture of a TV and ask them to repeat the word after you. Invite a student to come up. Motion for him or her to mimic your actions as you pretend to watch TV. Model the sentence: *He is watching TV.* Act out the following verbs in the same manner with a student: *eating, sleeping, reading.*

Model these sentences and ask students to repeat: *He is eating. They are sleeping. She is reading. They are watching TV.* Hold up the corresponding Picture Card as they say each sentence. Students who are acting out the verbs respond, and the rest of the class listens.

Now invite two or three students to act out a verb after you whisper it to them. Point to these students and ask the rest of the class: *What are they doing?* Model sentences: *They are*

eating. They are sleeping. They are reading. They are watching TV.

Tell students to use *he* or *she* when one person is doing an action right now and to use *they* when more than one person is doing an action right now.

USING PAGE 49

Help students find page 49 in their books. Ask students to tell what they see. Play the recording or read the Grammar Box as students follow along. Point to each picture as you read. Ask students to read chorally. Tell students that these sentences show actions that are happening now. Tell them that we say *he/she is* when

one person is doing an action. We say *they are* when we are talking about two or more people doing an action.

Read the directions for the writing activity with students. Point to the picture in number 1. Help them read the sentence: *He is watching TV.* Students trace the words to complete the sentence. Now ask students: *What are they doing?* as you point to the picture in number 2. Model the response: *They are reading.* Model how to write the word *reading* on the line to complete the sentence. Read chorally with students. Complete the rest of the page in the same manner with students. Read each sentence with them.

Using Page 50

Help students find page 50 in their books. Read each word in the word list as you hold up the corresponding Picture Card. Ask students to read with you. Now show them how to find the words in the word search puzzle. Show students how to circle each word. After they have circled the words, ask students to read and spell the words with you.

Now read the directions for the writing activity with students. Point to each corresponding picture and ask students to tell what action they see. Help them decide which pronoun to use to talk about the sentence. Now read the incomplete sentence with the class. Help students decide which word best finishes the sentence. Model writing the word on the line to complete the sentence. Complete the page with students.

HAVING FUN!
Charades

Write the following words on slips of paper ahead of time: *eating, sleeping, reading, watching.* Show students each word and practice reading with them. Now fold up the pieces of paper and place them in a box. Invite students to come up, choose a piece of paper, read it silently, and then act out the verb for the rest of the class. The student who guesses correctly first gets to act out the next verb. Students can answer using just the verb in the present progressive. For students with limited English ability, whisper the word to them and then ask them to act it out.

Listen and Do

Ask students to form a line from the front to the back of the room. Whisper one of these verbs to the first student: *reading, sleeping, eating, watching.* Motion for this student to whisper it to the next student in line. Students continue whispering the verb until the last student is reached. This student then acts out the verb and says it. The first student verifies if it is correct. Change students' places in line so that everyone gets a chance to be either the first or last student during the game.

Simon Says

Model the activity for students. Say: *Simon says (sleeping).* Students act out *(sleeping).* If you do not say *Simon Says,* students do nothing. Use the verbs: *reading, sleeping, eating, watching TV.* Encourage students to say the verb as they are acting it out.

Memory Game

Place the following Picture Cards faceup on the floor or on the table in front of students: *kitchen, living room, bedroom, bathroom, lamp, chair, table, picture, box, tub, bed, clock, read, sleep, eat, watch.* Point to each Picture Card and ask: *What is this?* Model responses if necessary. Now turn the cards facedown. Say: *Where is the (clock)?* Students take turns turning over one card. If they find the correct card, they keep it. The student with the most cards at the end of the game wins. Encourage students to name the pictures they turn over as they are playing.

A. Find and circle.

reading   eating   sleeping   watching

B. Write.

1. She is reading.
2. They are eating.
3. He is watching TV.
4. She is sleeping.

50 UNIT 5 | My House

Vocabulary: bathroom, bedroom, eat, kitchen, living room, read, sleep, they, TV, watch, we

Lesson Objectives
✓ to name household items
✓ to name rooms in the house
✓ to use prepositions *in, on, under*
✓ to use verbs in the present progressive tense
✓ to use subject pronouns *I, they*
✓ to use the subject pronoun *it* instead of a noun

Classroom English
• Draw. Show me. Find. Say. What is it?

Language Patterns
• They're (in) the (living room).
• They're (sleeping).

Materials
• **Picture Cards:** living room, bedroom, kitchen, bathroom, read, sleep, eat, watch

🎧 **Chant.**

He's in the living room.
He's reading.
He's reading.

They're in the living room.
They're reading.
They're reading.

She's in the bedroom.
She's sleeping.
She's sleeping.

They're in the bedroom.
They're sleeping.
They're sleeping.

they're = they are

Prepositions, *Where ...?*, Present Progressive ⑤①

WARMING UP

Review the rooms in the house with students. Hold up a Picture Card and ask students to tell what they see. Review verbs in the present progressive tense. Hold up a Picture Card and ask students to act it out. Tell what they are doing: *They are (sleeping).* Now hold up a picture of the other rooms. Model sentences that combine the verb in the present progressive and the room: *(They) are (eating) in the (kitchen).*

USING PAGE 51

Help students find page 51 in their books. Show the Picture Cards for rooms in the house and ask students to identify each one. Show them the Picture Cards for the verbs: *read, sleep, eat, watch.* Ask students to identify each verb. Read the chant and hold up the corresponding

Picture Cards so students have a better understanding of what the chant is about.

Tell students that we can change *they are* to *they're.* Show students that we omit the letter *a* and use an apostrophe for the word *they're.*

Model how students should act out each verb. Now ask students to say the first stanza of the chant with you. Hold up the card for *living room.*

Now divide the class into two groups. Ask group 1 to act out *reading.* Hold up the *living room* card as a prompt. Read the chant and ask the students in group 2 to follow along. Then ask them to say the chant with you and point to the students who are acting out what is happening. Now ask

groups to switch parts. Repeat this stanza of the chant. Continue in this manner, presenting the last two stanzas of the chant.

EXTENSION
Continue the Chant

Review the chant with students by playing the recording or reading it for them. Substitute other rooms and verbs in the present progressive. Hold up Picture Cards as prompts. Students say the new chant and act it out.

USING PAGE 52

Help students find page 52 in their books. Ask them to tell what they see. Ask: *Where is the (table)?* Show students how to find the hidden pictures. Ask them to find and color the table, chair, tub, clock, lamp, bed, picture, and box. After students have found all the items, do a Show Me activity with them. Ask: *Where is the (tub)? Show me.* Model. Students point to the items and name them.

Find and color.

table   chair   tub   clock   lamp   bed   picture   box

52 UNIT 5 | My House

Unit 6

Pets

Is it a ... ?, Have, You

Vocabulary: bird, cat, fish, frog, mouse, rabbit, snake, turtle

Lesson Objectives
✓ to name pets
✓ to ask, answer, and write questions with *is* and *isn't*

Classroom English
• Find. Say. Color. Draw. Listen. Write. Show me. What is this? What is it?

Language Patterns
• Is it a (bird)?
• Yes, it is.
• No, it isn't.

Materials
• drawing paper; pencils; crayons; bingo grids with nine spaces, one for each child; nine bingo markers for each child
• **Realia:** toy animals: cat, bird, frog, fish, turtle, mouse, rabbit, snake
• **Picture Cards:** cat, bird, frog, fish, turtle, mouse, rabbit, snake

WARMING UP

If available, place toy animals for the following words at the front of the classroom: *cat, bird, frog, fish, turtle, mouse, rabbit, snake.* If realia is not available, use Picture Cards.

Hold up the *(cat).* Model the word for students and ask them to repeat. After students have practiced the new vocabulary a few times, play a Show Me game. Give directions such as: *Show me the (cat).* Invite individual students to come up and point to the animal you name. Ask: *What is it?* Model responses if necessary and ask students to repeat chorally: *It is a (cat).*

Hold up the cat and ask: *Is it a bird?* Model shaking your head *no,* and ask students to repeat: *No, it isn't.* Practice this question and response for the other animal vocabulary. Hold

up the turtle and ask: *Is it a turtle?* Model shaking your head *yes,* and ask students to repeat: *Yes, it is.* Practice this question and response for the other animal vocabulary. Repeat the procedure, but this time write the question and responses on the board and read with students.

USING PAGE 53

Help students find page 53 in their books. Students identify what they see. Point to the items in the picture and ask: *What is it?* Model responses if necessary. Point to each item and word and play the recording or read each one for students. Students repeat. Play a Show Me game with students. Say: *Show me the (turtle).* Students point to the *(turtle).*

Continue practicing each word on the page.

Tell students: *Draw an orange circle around the cat.* Continue with different colors for each of the animals.

USING PAGE 54

Help students find page 54 in their books. Play the recording or read the Grammar Box as you point to the pictures. Students read with you. Explain that we say *Yes, it is* for affirmative answers and *No, it isn't* for negative answers.

Tell students that we can change *is not* to *isn't*. Show students that we omit the letter *o* and use an apostrophe for the word *isn't*.

Now read the directions for the writing activity. Students follow along. Point to each picture. Read the questions and answers for numbers 1 and 2. Ask students to write the questions and answers by tracing them. Help students fill in the missing words to complete the question in number 3. Then help them answer the question about the picture. Ask them to write the words. Use a similar procedure to complete the page with students. Read each completed question and answer with students. Assign the question to one student and the response to a second student. Model if necessary.

HAVING FUN!
Paired Questions

Students work in pairs. Give each student a Picture Card to hold behind their backs so their partner can't see it. Students take turns asking questions about their partner's cards and offering responses: *Is it a (cat)? Yes, it is. No, it isn't.* Students continue until they guess what Picture Card their partner is holding.

Animal Sounds

Hold up one of the Picture Cards and make the sound for that animal. Ask students to make the sound with you. After they have practiced making the sounds, play a Show Me game. Say the sound that the animal makes.

Students point to the corresponding Picture Card. Encourage students to name the animal as they point to it. Advanced level students can respond with complete sentences: *It is a (frog).*

Drawing Dictation

Give students a piece of drawing paper and show them how to fold it into eight boxes. Show them how to number the boxes from 1–8. Give students crayons. Give the following directions:

1. Draw a yellow fish.

Continue with different colors for each animal.

Advanced level students can label the pictures or write simple sentences

such as: *It is a (snake). It is a (green) (snake).*

Animal Bingo

Prepare bingo grids with nine spaces for each student. Use paper clips or small pieces of paper for markers. Give each student a grid. Tell students that everyone's bingo grid should be different. Ask students to draw animals in the spaces on their grid. Play bingo. Call out animal names. Students place markers on the animal pictures. Three in a row wins. The winner names each animal in his or her winning row. Advanced level students can respond with complete sentences: *It is a (rabbit).*

Vocabulary: bird, cat, fish, frog, mouse, rabbit, snake, turtle

Lesson Objectives
✓ to name pets

✓ to use *have*

✓ to use *do* and *don't*

Classroom English
• Cut. Show me. Write. Draw. Find. Listen. Say. Simon Says. What is it?

Language Patterns
• Do you have a (frog)?

• Yes, I do. No, I don't.

Materials
• pictures of animals with labels: *cat, bird, frog, fish, turtle, mouse, rabbit, snake*; drawing paper; construction paper; yardstick; string; paper clip; double-sided tape; magazines with pictures of animals to cut out; scissors; glue

• **Realia:** toy animals: cat, frog, fish, turtle, mouse, rabbit, snake

• **Picture Cards:** cat, frog, fish, turtle, mouse, rabbit, snake

WARMING UP

Review animal names with students. Hold up a Picture Card and ask: *What is it?* Model responses if necessary: *It is a (frog).* Ask them to talk about their favorite pets.

Give each student a piece of drawing paper and ask them to draw a cat. When they are finished ask: *Do you have a cat?* Motion for students to nod their heads *yes* and model the response: *Yes, I do.* Ask students to repeat. Now ask: *Do you have a turtle?* Motion for them to shake their heads *no* and model the response: *No, I don't.* Ask students to repeat.

Invite individual students to come up and choose a Picture Card. Ask: *Do you have a (fish)?* Students answer either *Yes, I do.* or *No, I*

don't. Model if necessary. Repeat the procedure, but this time have the class ask the question.

Write the question: *Do you have a frog?* on the board for students and ask them to repeat. Invite a student to come up and hold the frog Picture Card. Model the response: *Yes, I do.* and write it on the board. Ask: *Do you have a mouse?* Model the response: *No, I don't.* Write this on the board and then read each question and answer with students. Invite individual students to come up, read, and trace the words.

USING PAGE 55

Help students find page 55 in their books. Ask students to tell what they

see. Play the recording or read the Grammar Box as students follow along. Point to each character as you read. Ask them to read chorally. Explain that we can use short answers when we respond to questions.

Read the directions for the next exercise with students. Show them a picture of a pet you have drawn and labeled. Say: *It is a (cat).* Now ask students to draw a picture of a pet. When they are finished, ask individual students to hold up their pictures as you ask the rest of the class: *What is it?* Model responses if necessary and ask individuals to respond: *It is a (cat).*

USING PAGE 56

Help students find page 56 in their books. Ask them to read the directions with you. Ask students to look at the picture in number 1 and to tell what they see. Model reading the question and answer and ask students to read chorally. Students then trace the words.

Ask students to tell what they see in number 2. Help them read the word *turtle* and the answer: *No, I don't.* Model the question and ask students to say it with you. Show students how to write the question. Use a similar procedure for number 3.

Ask students to read the directions for Exercise B with you. Students identify the animal in the picture in number 1. Read the question and ask them to repeat. Read the response and ask them to trace the words.

Ask students to identify the animal in number 2. Read the question with students and help them answer it correctly: *Yes, I do.* Students write the answer. Use a similar procedure for number 3.

A. Write the questions.

1.

Do you have a rabbit?

Yes, I do. (rabbit)

2.

Do you have a turtle?

No, I don't. (turtle)

3.

Do you have a mouse?

Yes, I do. (mouse)

B. Write the answers.

1. Do you have a snake?

No, I don't.

2. Do you have a cat?

Yes, I do

3. Do you have a bird?

No, I don't.

HAVING FUN!
Fishing for Pets

Draw simple pictures of the animals in this lesson on construction paper and label them. Cut out the pictures and place them on the floor in front of students. Make a fishing pole from a yardstick or other long stick by tying a string to the end and then taping a large paper clip to the string. (This is the hook.) Place some double-sided tape on the paper clip. Invite students to go fishing. Model the activity. Say: *Do you have a (cat)?* The student responds: *No, I don't.* Then ask the student to go fishing for the (cat). Students catch the animal by placing the tape on the picture and fishing it off the floor. After students have caught their animals ask: *Do you*

have a (cat)? Help them respond: *Yes, I do.* Continue playing until each student has had a turn to catch an animal.

Paired Questions

Model the activity. Students work in pairs. Students choose a Picture Card to hold behind their backs so their partner can't see it. Students take turns asking questions about their partner's cards, to determine the animal: *Do you have a (cat)?* Students respond with an affirmative or negative short answer: *Yes, I do.* or *No, I don't.*

Pet Collage

Bring in old magazines that have animals in them for students to cut

out pictures of pets. Show students a finished collage for them to use as a model. Point to pictures of animals from this lesson and ask them to tell what they see. If possible, use pictures of people with animals and ask: *What is it?* Model short affirmative and negative answers if necessary and ask students to reply.

Animal Simon Says

Play Animal Simon Says with students. Model the activity. When you say: *Simon says, mouse.* Students act like a mouse. If you don't say *Simon Says,* students do nothing. Use animals from this lesson.

Vocabulary: bird, fish, frog, mouse, rabbit, snake, turtle

Lesson Objectives
✓ to name pets

✓ to use *have/has*

✓ to use pronouns *he* and *she*

Classroom English
- Say. Write. Find. Show me. What is it? What does (he/she) have?
- He/She has a (turtle).

Language Patterns
- What does he have? What does she have?
- He has a (frog). She has a (frog).

Materials
- box or bag; drawing paper; crayons; slips of paper with animal names: *bird, frog, fish, turtle, mouse, rabbit, snake*
- **Realia:** toy animals: cat, bird, frog, fish, turtle, mouse, rabbit, snake
- **Picture Cards:** bird, frog, fish, turtle, mouse, rabbit, snake

WARMING UP

Review animal names with students. Hold up a Picture Card and ask: *What is it?* Model responses if necessary: *It is a (frog).*

Invite a boy in your class to come up and hold one of the toy animals or an animal Picture Card. Model the question: *What does he have?* Invite students to respond using language they know. One word answers are acceptable.

Model the full sentence response: *He has a (frog).* Ask students to repeat after you. Use a similar procedure to practice other sentences such as: *He has a (turtle).* Now invite a girl in your class to come up and repeat the procedure using *she.*

Write the questions and answers you practiced with students on the board and ask them to read with you. Invite individual students to come up, read, and trace the words to write the questions and answers.

USING PAGE 57

Help students find page 57 in their books. Play the recording or read the Grammar Box with students. Ask students to follow along and read with you. Point to the pictures as you read. Explain that the question uses the word *have* and the answer for *he* and *she* uses the word *has.*

Read the directions for the writing activity with students. Point to each picture and ask students to tell what they see. Point to Sam in number 1 and ask: *What does he have?* Elicit responses and model if necessary. Read the question and answer with students. Now ask students to trace and write the missing words in each question and answer. Use a similar procedure to complete numbers 2 and 3. As you work with students, write answers on the board as a model for them to follow. Students read, trace, and complete the sentences.

USING PAGE 58

Help students find page 58 in their books. Read the directions for Exercise A with them. Point to the picture in number 1 and ask students to tell what they see. Point to Sam and ask: *What does he have?* Elicit responses and model if necessary. Read the answer with students: *He has a mouse.* Ask students to trace the words to the answer.

Point to Maria and ask: *What does she have?* Elicit responses and model if necessary. Write the answer on the board and read it with students. Ask them to write the answer. Use a similar procedure to complete number 3.

Read the directions for Exercise B with students. Point to Maria and ask: *What does she have?* Elicit responses and model if necessary. Read the answer: *She has a turtle.* Ask students to trace the words to write the question.

Point to Sam in number 2. Ask students to tell what he has. Help students write the question: *What does he have?* on the line. Read the response: *He has a snake.* Use a similar procedure to complete number 3.

HAVING FUN!
Animal Charades

Write the animal names on slips of paper ahead of time. Place the slips of paper in a box or bag. Model the activity. Students choose a slip of paper, read it, and then act out what the animal does. Help beginning-level students read the animal names by whispering the words to them. The student who guesses correctly first gets to act out the next animal.

Animals in Sequence

Place the animal Picture Cards from this lesson on the floor or on the board in front of students. Quickly

review the vocabulary with them. Model the activity. Say three animal names. Students come up, point to, and say the animal names in the order you said them.

What's Missing?

Place the animal Picture Cards on the floor in front of students. Ask them to close their eyes. Take away one Picture Card. When they open their eyes, point to the space where the missing card should be and ask them to tell what is missing. The student who guesses correctly first gets to take away the next card.

Ask and Answer

Model the following conversation for students:

Student 1: *What does (he/she) have?*
Student 2: *(He/She) has a (turtle).*
A third student holds the toy turtle or Picture Card of the turtle.

Give students a chance to take all three parts.

Guessing Game

Place the Picture Cards faceup on the floor or on a table in front of students and ask them to name each animal. Encourage them to use complete sentences such as: *It is a (turtle).* Turn the cards facedown and ask: *Where is the (rabbit)?* Invite students to take turns turning over one card to find the animal you name. If students guess correctly, they keep the card. The student with the most cards at the end of the game wins.

Vocabulary: bird, cat, fish, frog, mouse, rabbit, snake, turtle

Lesson Objectives

✓ to name pets

✓ to ask questions with *have*

✓ to use affirmative and negative short answers

Classroom English

• Draw. Show me. Find. Say. What is it? What does he/she have? Is it a (cat)? Yes, it is. No, it isn't.

Language Patterns

• What does (he/she) have? (He/She) has a (turtle).

• Is it a (snake)? Yes, it is. No, it isn't.

Materials

• **Picture Cards:** cat, bird, frog, fish, turtle, mouse, rabbit, snake

WARMING UP

Review animal names from this lesson. Hold up a Picture Card and ask: *What is this?* Students respond: *It is a (snake).* Ask questions such as: *Is it a (mouse)? Do you have a (turtle)?* as you hold up Picture Cards as prompts. Model responses if necessary.

USING PAGE 59

Help students find page 59 in their books. Show them the Picture Cards of pets and ask them to identify the animals. Hold up the *mouse* and ask: *Is it a mouse?* Students reply: *Yes, it is.* Now ask: *Is it a snake?* Students reply: *No, it isn't.*

Act out the chant by holding or pointing to the appropriate Picture Card as you say the chant. Play the recording or read the chant for students. Model and ask students to follow along and point to each word as they listen. After students have listened to and read the chant a few

🎧 **Chant.**

What does she have?
Is it a cat?
Yes, it is.
Yes, it is.

What does she have?
Is it a snake?
Yes, it is.
Yes, it is.

What does she have?
Is it a frog?
Yes, it is.
Yes, it is.

Is it a ...?, Have, You 59

times, invite them to say it with you. Encourage them to point to each word as they read and then to find the corresponding picture to each stanza.

EXTENSION
Continue the Chant

Review the chant with students by playing the recording or reading it for them. Substitute other pets. Hold up Picture Cards as prompts. Students say the new chant and act it out. You can also substitute a negative short answer: *No, it isn't.* for some new stanzas of the chant.

USING PAGE 60

Help students find page 60 in their books. Point to number 1 and ask: *What is it?* Help students identify the ear and which animal it belongs to (the cat). Model the response: *It is a cat.* Use a similar procedure for the other pictures. Students try to guess which animal the illustration represents.

EXTENSION
Ask and Answer

After students have identified all the animals, give them the opportunity to ask each other: *What is it?* as they point to different illustrations on the page. Encourage students to answer using complete sentences.

Students can also point to a picture and ask: *Is it a (cat)?* Their partner responds with either an affirmative or negative short answer.

Finish the Picture

Model the activity. Point to number 1 and ask: *What is it?* Students reply: *It is a cat.* Show them how to draw the rest of the cat to complete the picture. Students complete each drawing on the page.

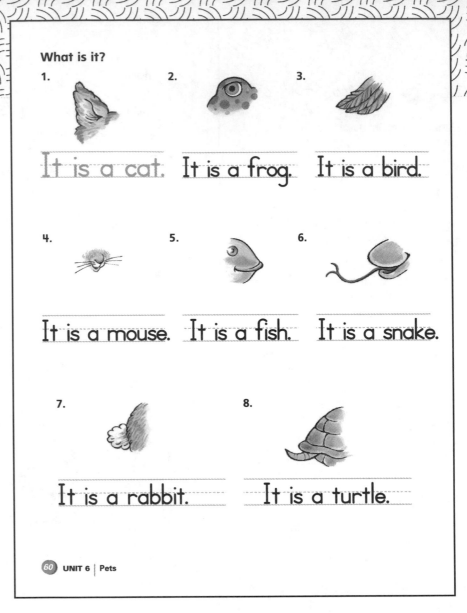

What is it?

1. It is a cat.

2. It is a frog.

3. It is a bird.

4. It is a mouse.

5. It is a fish.

6. It is a snake.

7. It is a rabbit.

8. It is a turtle.

60   UNIT 6 | Pets

Units 5 & 6
Review

Vocabulary: bird, box, cat, chair, clock, eat, fish, frog, lamp, mouse, picture, rabbit, read, sleep, snake, table, tub, turtle, watch

Review Objectives
✓ to name household items
✓ to name pets
✓ to use prepositions of place
✓ to use present progressive
✓ to use *have* and *has*

Classroom English
• Listen. Check. Color. Point. Say. It is a (rabbit). This is a (rabbit).

Language Patterns
• I am (eating).
• The (bird) is under the (table).
• (He) has a (cat).

Materials
• **Picture Cards:** rabbit, turtle, frog, mouse, cat, fish, snake, clock, lamp, picture, chair, table, box, tub, eat, sleep, read

WARMING UP

Review the vocabulary words from Units 4 and 5 with students. Use Picture Cards or realia. Ask: *What is it?* Invite students to use a complete sentence when answering: *It is a rabbit.*

Review prepositions with students. Place one of the Picture Cards or an item in a large box. Ask: *What is it?* Model the response if necessary and ask students to repeat: *It is a (turtle).* Now ask: *Where is the (turtle)?* Model the response if necessary and ask students to

repeat: *The turtle is (in) the box.* Provide additional opportunities for students to tell where items are. Encourage them to use complete sentences and to use the prepositions *in, on,* and *under.* Use the Picture Cards for pets and household items. Invite a student to come up to the front of the room. Ask him or her to pick a Picture Card. Then ask the rest of the class: *What does (he/she) have?* Model the response if necessary and ask

students to repeat: *(He/She) has a chair.* Provide additional opportunities for students to tell what other classmates have.

Review present progressive sentences with students. Act out one of these verbs: *eating, sleeping, reading* and ask students to act it out with you.

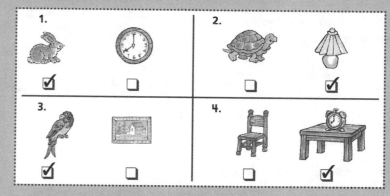

Review: Units 5 and 6

Vocabulary
🎧 **A. Listen and check.**

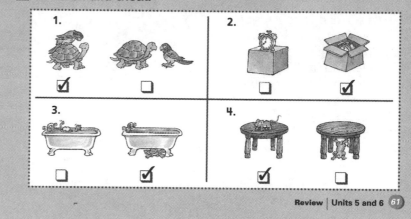

In, On, Under
🎧 **B. Listen and check.**

Review | Units 5 and 6 **61**

AUDIOSCRIPT

A. 1. rabbit   2. lamp   3. bird   4. table

B. 1. The bird is on the turtle.   2. The clock is in the box.   3. The frog is under the tub.   4. The mouse is on the table.

Ask: *What are you doing?* Model the response if necessary and ask students to repeat: *I am (eating).* Practice each verb with students.

If you feel students need to practice exercises that are similar to those presented in the Review Units, use exercises similar to the ones described for Review Units 1 and 2, Pages 25–26. Students can practice checking boxes and pictures that go with sentences and words they hear.

USING PAGE 61

Help students find page 61 in their books. Help students find Exercise A. Read the directions and ask students to follow along. Point to each picture and ask students to say the words with you. Explain that they should listen and check the picture that goes with the word they hear. Play the recording or read the audioscript for students. Students check the correct picture.

Help students find Exercise B. Read the directions and ask them to follow along. Point to the pictures and ask students to tell where the pets or items are. Explain that students should check the box that goes with the sentence they hear. Play the recording or read the audioscript. Students check the correct picture.

USING PAGE 62

Help students find page 62 in their books. Help students find Exercise C. Read the directions and ask them to follow along. Explain to students that

they should check the box that goes with the sentence they hear. Play the recording or read the audioscript for students. Students mark the correct picture.

Help students find Exercise D. Read the directions and ask them to follow along. Explain that they should listen, point to the pictures, and say the sentences. Play the recording or read the audioscript. Students repeat.

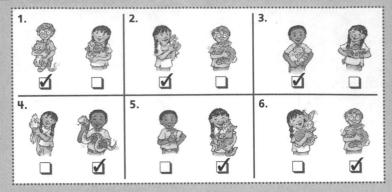

Review: Units 5 and 6

Have
🎧 **C. Listen and check.**

Present Progressive
🎧 **D. Listen, point, and say.**

62 Review | Units 5 and 6

AUDIOSCRIPT

C. 1. He has a cat.   2. She has a mouse.   3. He has a fish.   4. He has a snake.

     5. She has a cat.   6. He has a rabbit.

D. 1. They are eating.   2. We are watching TV.   3. They are sleeping.   4. We are reading.

Unit 7
Happy Birthday!

How old ... ?, His/Her, Whose ... ?

Vocabulary: balloon, cake, camera, candle, candy, card, game, ice cream, present

Lesson Objectives
✓ to name items found at a birthday party
✓ to ask, answer, and write *How old are you?*
✓ to count to ten

Classroom English
• Find. Say. Color. Draw. Listen. Write. Show me. What is this? What is it?

Language Patterns
• How old are you? I'm (6) years old.

Materials
• drawing paper; pencils; crayons; a camera to take students' pictures; a box wrapped to look like a present; wrap only the lid; poster board
• **Realia:** present, balloon, greeting card, candle, camera, candy, a game
• **Picture Cards:** cake, present, balloon, card, ice cream, candle, camera, candy, game

WARMING UP

If available bring in the following items: *a present, a balloon, a game, a greeting card, a candle, a camera, candy.* Place all of the items in a box so students can't see. Allow them to feel what is inside the box without looking. After everyone has felt what is in the box, ask students to tell what is in the box. Since the vocabulary is new for students, allow them to answer using gestures or their native language.

Take out each item or show the Picture Cards. Model how to say each word and ask students to repeat with you. Explain that these items are used at a birthday party.

Draw a picture of a boy and a birthday cake with seven candles on it. Hold up the picture of the cake and count the candles. Point to the boy and say: *He is 7 years old.* Point to yourself and say: *I am (29) years old.* Ask students: *How old are you?* Model the response for them: *I am (7) years old.* and ask them to say it with you.

USING PAGE 63

Help students find page 63 in their books. Students identify what they see. Point to items in the pictures and ask: *What is this?* Model responses if necessary. Point to each item and play the recording or read. Students repeat. Play a Show Me game with students. Say: *Show me the (cake).* Students point to the (cake). Continue practicing each word on the page.

Give the following directions and complete the page with students:

Draw a yellow circle around the card.

Continue with different colors for each vocabulary word.

USING PAGE 64

Help students find page 64 in their books. Play the recording or read the Grammar Box as you point to the pictures. Students read with you. Now read the directions for Exercise A. Point to each picture. Read the question and answer for number 1. Ask students to trace the question and answer. Point to the line in number 2, help students see that the question is missing, and ask them to write it. Read the answer with the class. Use a similar procedure to complete number 3.

Tell students that we can change *I am* to *I'm*. Show students that we omit the letter *a* and use an apostrophe for the word *I'm*.

Read the directions for Exercise B. Help students read the question and then ask individuals to answer it about themselves. Help students write and answer the question. Write a model on the board for students to use as a reference.

HAVING FUN!

Is it a (camera)?

Use realia or Picture Cards for this activity. Model how the game is played. Wrap up a box top to look like a present. Place one of the items or Picture Cards in the box without letting students see what it is. Model the activity. Students ask questions to guess what is inside: *Is it a (camera)?* Respond with the short answer: *Yes, it is.* or *No, it isn't.* The student who guesses correctly first gets to place the next item or Picture Card in the box and answer the students' questions. Model responses if necessary.

Drawing Dictation

Give students a piece of drawing paper and show them how to fold it into eight boxes. Give students

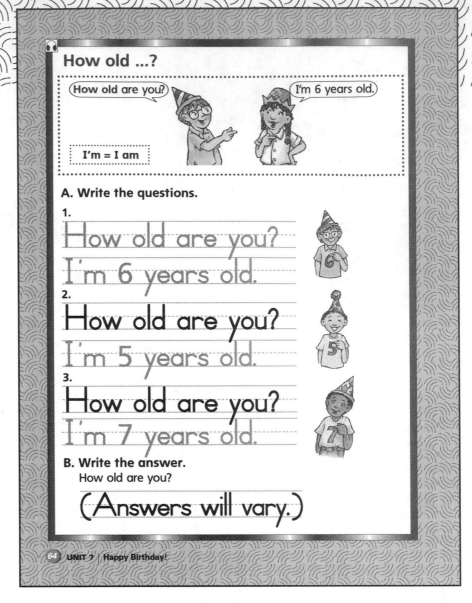

crayons. Show them how to number the boxes from 1–8. Give the following directions:

1. Draw a yellow candle.

Continue with different colors for each object. Advanced students can label the pictures or write simple sentences such as: *It is a (candle). It is a (yellow) (candle).*

Students' Pictures

Take pictures of students if a camera is available, or ask students to draw pictures of themselves. Ask students to write their names and how old they are on a separate strip of paper. Display their pictures and sentences by pasting them on poster board or making a bulletin board display. Allow

students time at the beginning or end of each class to talk about each other's pictures and to tell how old they are.

Guessing Game

Place the Picture Cards in a pile and cover the first picture with a piece of paper. Ask: *What is it?* Slowly begin to lift the piece of paper so students can see a little bit of the picture. Continue to lift the paper until someone can guess what the picture is. Encourage students to respond using a complete sentence: *It is a (candle).*

Vocabulary: balloon, cake, camera, candle, candy, card, game, ice cream, present

Lesson Objectives
✓ to name items found at a birthday party
✓ to use possessives *his* and *her*

Classroom English
• Say. Write. Find. Show me. This is his/her (cake).

Language Patterns
• This is his (present).
• This is her (balloon).

Materials
• drawing paper; crayons; balloons with students' names on slips of paper inside
• **Realia:** present, balloon, greeting card, candle, camera, candy, game
• **Picture Cards:** cake, present, balloon, card, ice cream, candle, camera, candy, game

WARMING UP

Ask students to draw a picture of a balloon and to put their names on it. Collect the pictures, hold them up one by one and say: (*Greg*). *This is his balloon.* Emphasize the word *his* as you say each sentence. Give (Greg) his balloon picture. Hand out the boy's pictures first. Write the word *his* on the board and read it with students. Explain to students that when something belongs to a man or boy we use the word *his*.

Use a similar procedure for the girls' pictures. Explain to students that when something belongs to a woman or a girl, we use the word *her*.

USING PAGE 65

Help students find page 65 in their books. Play the recording or read the Grammar Box with students. Ask

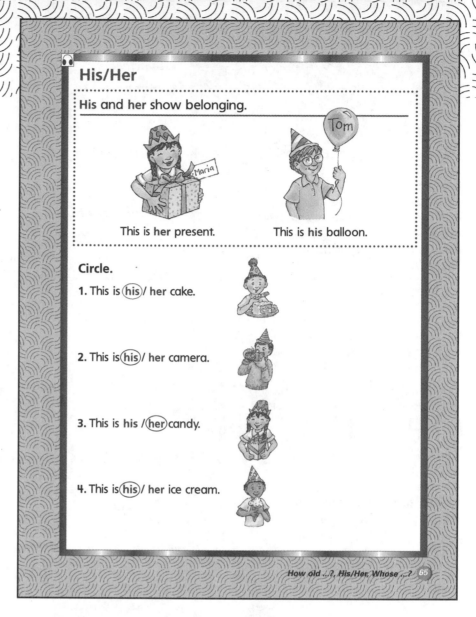

His/Her

His and her show belonging.

This is **her** present.   This is **his** balloon.

Circle.

1. This is (his)/ her cake.

2. This is (his)/ her camera.

3. This is his /(her) candy.

4. This is (his)/ her ice cream.

them to follow along and read with you. Point to the pictures as you read.

Read the directions for the activity with students. Point to each picture and ask students to tell who and what they see. Read each sentence with students and ask them to circle the correct word to complete the sentence about the picture. Ask students to trace the circle in number 1 and to read the sentence chorally. Use a similar procedure to complete each sentence with students. When the page is complete, read each sentence again and ask for volunteers to read for the class.

USING PAGE 66

Help students find page 66 in their books. Read the directions for Exercise A with them. Point to each picture and ask students to tell who and what they see. Then ask students to tell who the item in the picture belongs to. Model sentences such as: *This is his card.*

Now read the first sentence with students and help them find the matching picture. Ask them to trace the line from the first sentence to the third picture. Use a similar procedure to complete this exercise.

Read the directions for Exercise B with students. Point to the picture in number 1 and ask students to tell who and what they see. Ask them to tell who the camera belongs to. Model the response: *This is her camera.* Ask students to repeat. Read the sentence and ask students to trace the word.

Point to the picture in number 2. After students have identified who the ice cream belongs to, model the sentence: *This is his ice cream.* Read the first two words in the sentence and ask students to read with you. Now ask them to tell you which word is missing. Elicit that *his* is missing. Ask students to write the missing word on the line. Use a similar procedure to complete number 3.

HAVING FUN!
Make a Birthday Card

Show students a completed birthday card and talk about the pictures and words you wrote inside. Make it available to students as they work to use as a model.

Give each student a piece of drawing paper and show them how to fold it to make a card. Ask them to draw a cake on the front. Show them how to write *Happy Birthday!* inside and to

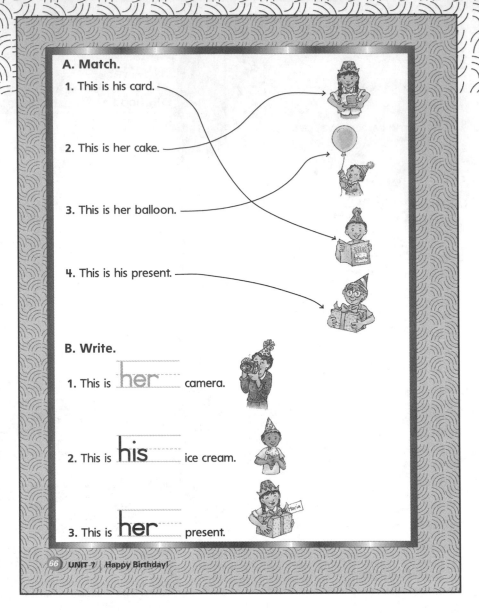

A. Match.

1. This is his card.

2. This is her cake.

3. This is her balloon.

4. This is his present.

B. Write.

1. This is **her** camera.

2. This is **his** ice cream.

3. This is **her** present.

66 UNIT 7 | Happy Birthday!

draw another party picture. When they are finished, invite them to share their cards with the rest of the class. They can talk about their pictures and read the words *Happy Birthday!*

Collect the students' cards. Hold up each one and ask the class who it belongs to. Invite volunteers to point to the owner and say: *This is (his/her) card.*

Names in Balloons

Write students' names on small slips of paper ahead of time and place them in balloons. Blow up the balloons. Give each student a balloon. Help them pop the balloons one at a time. Help students read the name that is inside the balloon. Students

then go to the person whose name they have and say: *This is his/her name.*

Guessing Game

Place the party Picture Cards faceup on the floor or on a table in front of students and ask them to name each item. Encourage them to use complete sentences such as: *It is a (cake).* Turn the cards facedown and ask: *Where is the (cake)?* Invite students to take turns turning over one card to find the item you name. If students guess correctly, they keep the card. The student with the most cards at the end of the game wins.

Vocabulary: balloon, cake, camera, candle, candy, card, game, ice cream, present

Lesson Objectives
✓ to name items found at a birthday party
✓ to ask, answer, and write *Whose (present) is this? It's (his/her) (present).*
✓ to use *his* and *her*

Classroom English
• Show me. Write. Draw. Put. Find. Listen. Say. Simon Says. What is this/that? Do you have a (frog)? Yes, I do. No, I don't

Language Patterns
• Whose (present) is this?
• It's (her/his) present.

Materials
• drawing paper, double-sided tape, big box, magazines with pictures of food items and people, poster board, glue, beanbag
• **Picture Cards:** cake, present, balloon, card, ice cream, candle, camera, candy, game

Whose ...?

Whose present is this?

It's her present.

It's = It is

Write the question.

1.
Whose ice cream is this?
It's her ice cream.

2.
Whose card is this?
It's his card.

3.
Whose camera is this?
It's her camera.

4.
Whose balloon is this?
It's his balloon.

WARMING UP

Give each student a piece of drawing paper and ask them to draw a candle. When they are finished, collect their pictures. Hold up one of the pictures and ask: *Whose candle is this?* After the student has claimed his or her picture, ask the class to respond: *This is (his/her) candle.* Use a similar procedure as you hold up each picture.

Now invite students to come up, choose a picture, and ask the question: *Whose candle is this?* Ask the class to respond: *This is (his/her) candle.*

Draw a picture of a boy with a candle and a girl with a candle on the board ahead of time. Point to each picture

and ask: *Whose candle is this?* Write the question on the board and read it with students. Write the responses: *This is his candle. This is her candle.* Read with students. Ask volunteers to come up, read the questions and answers, and trace the words.

USING PAGE 67

Help students find page 67 in their books. Ask students to tell what they see. Play the recording or read the Grammar Box for students as they follow along. Point to each character as you read. Ask students to read chorally. Explain that we use the question word *whose* when we want to ask to whom an item belongs.

Tell students that we can change *It is* to *It's.* Show students that we omit

the letter *i* and use an apostrophe for the word *It's.*

Read the directions for the exercise with students. Point to the picture in number 1 and ask them to tell who and what they see. Ask: *Whose ice cream is this?* Elicit: *It's her ice cream.* Read the question and answer with students.

Point to the picture in number 2 and ask students to tell who and what they see. Ask: *Whose card is this?* Elicit: *It's his card.* Now point to the line and ask students to tell what is missing. Help them see that the question is missing. Invite a volunteer to say the question. Students write the question on the line. Use a similar procedure to complete numbers 3 and 4.

USING PAGE 68

Help students find page 68 in their books. Ask them to read the directions with you. Ask students to look at the picture in number 1 and to tell who and what they see. Ask: *Whose candy is this?* Elicit: *It's her candy.* Read the question and answer with students.

Point to the picture in number 2. Students tell who and what they see. Ask: *Whose present is this?* Elicit: *It's his present.* Read the question. Ask students to look at the answer and tell which word is missing. Elicit: *It's* and tell students to fill it in. Use a similar procedure to complete the rest of the page.

HAVING FUN!
Put the Candles on the Cake

Draw a picture of a boy or girl on the board ahead of time. Draw a big birthday cake on a large piece of drawing paper ahead of time. Tape this to the board. Draw and cut out birthday candles. Place double-sided tape on the back of each candle. You should have one for each student. Students come up one at a time, close their eyes, spin around three times, and then try to place a candle on the cake without looking. After everyone has had a turn, count the candles and ask students to tell how old this boy or girl is.

Whose is this?

Ask each student to give you one object of theirs (a pencil, an eraser, a hair ribbon, etc.). Place all the objects in a big box. Model the activity. Take one object out and show it to the class. Ask: *Whose is this?* Ask students to look around and to try to figure out whose it is. The student who guesses correctly first gets to take out the next object and ask: *Whose is this?*

Write.

1. Whose candy is this?

   It's her candy.

2. Whose present is this?

   It's his present.

3. Whose balloon is this?

   It's her balloon.

4. Whose ice cream **is** this?

   It's his ice cream.

5. Whose card is **is this** ?

   It's his card.

Continue until all the objects have been returned.

Party Collage

Divide the class into groups of three or four. Give students old magazines that contain pictures of food items and people. Ask students to cut out pictures of party items and party activities. Students glue these pictures on large pieces of poster board. Advanced language learners can label their pictures.

When they are finished, ask each group to present their collages. Encourage students to name the pictures and, when possible, to show possession using *his* and *hers*. Prompt them with questions such as: *What is this? Whose (cake) is this?*

Party Game

Place the birthday Picture Cards on the floor in front of students. Model the activity. Students choose a word and then throw a beanbag at the picture. If the beanbag lands on the Picture Card, they get to keep it. If not, play goes to the next student. The player with the most cards at the end of the game wins. Encourage students to talk about their pictures by using gestures, sentence approximations, or complete sentences: *candle, a candle, It is a candle.*

Vocabulary: balloon, cake, camera, candle, candy, card, game, ice cream, present

Lesson Objectives
✓ to name items found at a birthday party
✓ to tell how old one is using *I'm, He's, She's*
✓ to say a birthday chant
✓ to use *his* and *hers*

Classroom English
• Draw a line. Show me. Find. Say. What is it? What does he/she have? It's (his/her) (balloon). Whose (cake) is it?

Language Patterns
• Whose (candle) is this? It's (his/her) candle.
• How old are you? I'm (6).
• It's (my/his/her) birthday. He's/She's (8).

Materials
• index cards, crayons
• **Picture Cards:** cake, present, balloon, card, ice cream, candle, camera, candy, game

🎧 Chant.

It's my birthday.
I'm 6.
I'm 6.

It's her birthday.
She's 10.
She's 10.

It's his birthday.
He's 8.
He's 8.

It's = It is
I'm = I am
She's = She is
He's = He is

How old ...?, His/Her, Whose ...? 69

WARMING UP

Begin by reviewing party items from this lesson. Hold up a Picture Card and ask: *What is this?* Students respond: *It is a (cake).*

Review asking and answering: *How old are you? I'm (6) years old.* Ask students to sit in a circle. Begin by asking the student on your right. After he or she answers, he or she asks the person on his or her right. Continue around the circle until everyone has had a chance.

Review questions with *whose*. Write each students' name on an index card. Hold it up and read the name if necessary. Ask: *Whose name is this?* Students point to the student whose

name you are holding and say: *It's (his/her) name.*

USING PAGE 69

Help students find page 69 in their books. Act out the chant by holding up the appropriate number of fingers as you say the chant. Play the recording or read the chant for students. Model and ask students to follow along and point to each word as they listen. After they have listened to and read the chant a few times, invite them to say it with you. Encourage students to point to each word as they read.

EXTENSION
Continue the Chant

Review the chant with students by playing the recording or reading it for them. Substitute other numbers, as you point to individual students. The rest of the class says the new chant and acts it out by pointing to the student and holding up the appropriate number of fingers.

Using Page 70

Help students find page 70 in their books. Model the activity. Point to number 1 and ask: *Who is this? What is this?* Students reply: *It is Tom. It's a balloon.* Ask: *Whose balloon is it?* Students reply: *It's his balloon.* Tell students to find Tom's balloon by drawing a line from Tom to the balloon on the other side of the page. Use a similar procedure to complete the rest of the page with students. When they are finished, ask them to color the pictures.

Extension

Students talk about the pictures they colored in the activity on page 70. Point to pictures and ask: *What's this?* Students respond using the color: *It's a (red) (balloon).* Model if necessary.

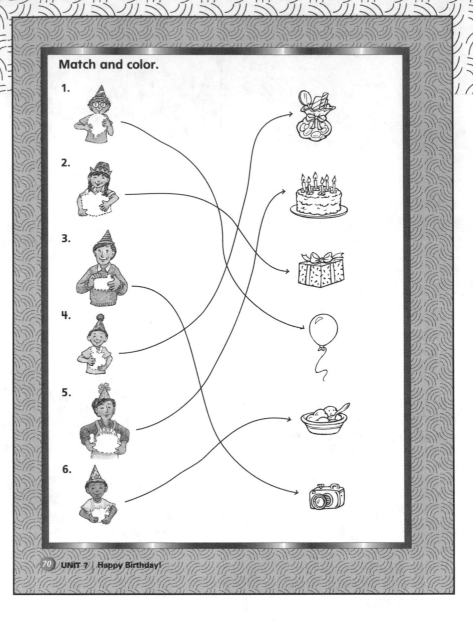

Match and color.

1.
2.
3.
4.
5.
6.

Unit 8
In the Toy Store

Do you like ... ?, Does he/she like ... ?, Do you want ... ?

Vocabulary: ball, boat, car, crayon, doll, kite, puzzle, train, yo-yo

Lesson Objective
✓ to name toys

Classroom English
• Find. Say. Color. Draw. Read. Show me. What is it? It is a (yo-yo).

Language Patterns
• What is it? It is a (train).
• What are they? They are (crayons).

Materials
• crayons
• **Realia:** doll, yo-yo, toy train, kite, toy car, ball, puzzle, crayons, toy boat
• **Picture Cards:** doll, yo-yo, train, kite, car, ball, puzzle, crayon, boat

WARMING UP

Bring in the following items or use Picture Cards: doll, yo-yo, toy train, kite, toy car, ball, puzzle, crayons, toy boat. Set up the items to look as if they are on a shelf in a toy store. Ask students to talk about the toys. Since this is new vocabulary, allow students to use gestures and their native language to tell what they see. Tell them they are in a pretend toy store.

Pick up a toy or a Picture Card and say the word or play the recording. Ask students to repeat. Use a similar procedure to practice each word. After students are familiar with the new vocabulary, ask: *What is this?* Model complete sentences and ask students to repeat: *It's a (kite).* Use a similar procedure to practice the rest of the vocabulary. Remind students of the plural forms of nouns and practice asking and answering: *What are they? They are crayons.*

Ask a student to come up and choose an item or a Picture Card. Ask the rest of the class to tell what he or she has: *He/She has a (train).* Invite other students to come up and participate.

USING PAGE 71

Help students find page 71 in their books. Play the recording or read the words as you point to each one. Students repeat. Ask students: *What is this?* as you point to key vocabulary.

Give the following directions and model the activity.
Teacher: *Draw a green circle around the crayons. Draw a blue circle around the doll.*

Continue with different colors for each vocabulary word. When students are finished, ask them to talk about the objects. Model sentences such as: *It is an orange kite. It is a yellow yo-yo.*

HAVING FUN!
Search and Find

Place the following toys or Picture Cards around the room ahead of time: doll, yo-yo, train, kite, car, ball, puzzle, crayons, boat. Ask: *Where is the (puzzle)?* Students walk around the room and search for the (puzzle). The student who finds it first is the winner. As students are playing ask: *What is this? What is that? Where is the (puzzle)?* Continue playing until all the toys have been found.

Vocabulary: ball(s), boat(s), car(s), crayon(s), doll(s), kite(s), puzzle(s), train(s), yo-yo(s)

Lesson Objectives
✓ to name toys
✓ to say, read, and write the question and answer pattern: *Does (he/she) like (cars)? No, (he/she) (does/doesn't).*
✓ to use singular and plural nouns

Classroom English
• Find. Say. Color. Show me. Read. Write. Draw. What is this? It is a (boat). What are they? They are (trains).

Language Patterns
• Does he/she like (cars)? Yes, he/she does. No, he/she doesn't.

Materials
• drawing paper, scissors, crayons, slips of paper with toy names written on them, box, ball
• **Realia:** puzzle
• **Picture Cards:** doll, yo-yo, train, kite, car, ball, puzzle, crayon, boat

WARMING UP

Show students the Picture Cards or the toys and review the new vocabulary with them. Ask: *What's this?* or *What are they?* Model responses if necessary and ask students to repeat.

Say the word *like* and act out its meaning by smiling and nodding. As you are doing this, point to one of the Picture Cards. Model the sentence: *I like (puzzles).* You should emphasize that this sentence uses the plural form of the noun. Now point to a different Picture Card or toy and shake your head to show *no.* Say the vocabulary word and say: *No. No, I don't.*

Hold up a Picture Card or a toy and ask students to tell what it is. Invite a student to come up. Ask: *Do you like*

(puzzles)? Help the student respond by nodding to show *yes,* or shaking his or her head to show *no.* Ask the rest of the class to respond to his or her gestures after you ask: *Does (he/she) like (crayons)?* Then model the response: *Yes, he/she does. No, he/she doesn't.* Role-play similar situations, questions, and responses with students.

USING PAGE 72

Help students find page 72 in their books. Play the recording or read the Grammar Box as you point to the pictures. Students read with you. Explain that we use the word *does* when we ask about other people, such as *he/she.* We can answer using short answers about other people:

Yes, he/she does. or *No, he/she doesn't.*

Read the directions for the writing activity as students follow along. Point to each picture and ask students to tell who and what they see and if the child likes what he or she has. Read the first question and answer and ask students to read with you and then to trace the words.

Read question 2 with students and tell them that some words are missing. Elicit that the words *Does she like* are missing. Students fill in the missing words to complete the question. Use a similar procedure to complete the rest of the page.

A. Write the answers.

1. Does he like boats?

Yes, he does.

2. Does she like cars?

No, she doesn't.

3. Does he like dolls?

No, he doesn't.

4. Does she like kites?

Yes, she does.

B. Write the questions.

1.

Does he like trains?

Yes, he does.   (trains)

2.

Does he like crayons?

Yes, he does.   (crayons)

3.

Does she like balls?

No, she doesn't.   (balls)

Do you like ...?, Does he/she like ...?, Do you want ...? 73

USING PAGE 73

Help students find page 73 in their books. Read the directions for Exercise A. Point to each picture and ask students to tell who they see, what they see, and if the person likes what they have.

Read the question in number 1 and point to the picture. Elicit the response: *Yes, he does.* and ask students to trace the words. Use a similar procedure to complete numbers 2–4. Students write the correct response.

Read the directions for Exercise B. Ask students to identify who and what they see and to tell if the person likes what he or she has. Read the first question and answer and point to the picture. Ask students to read with you and then to trace the words. Use a similar procedure to complete the rest of the page. Students write questions for each picture.

HAVING FUN!
Make Puzzles

Show students a finished puzzle. Take it apart and then show them how to assemble it. Give each student a piece of drawing paper. Ask them to draw their favorite toy all over the piece of paper. Explain that most of the paper should be covered with the picture. When students are finished, help them cut their paper into 6–8 pieces to make a puzzle. Invite two students to exchange and then assemble each other's puzzles. When they are finished, they can guess what their partner drew.

Act Out Playing

Write the toy names on slips of paper ahead of time. Place them in a box or small bag. Students come up and choose a slip of paper. Help students read the toy word. Students then act out which toy it is by showing how to play with it. The rest of the class guesses which toy it is. Prompt students with questions: *What is this?* The student who guesses correctly gets to choose the next slip of paper. Continue playing until all the toys have been guessed. After students have acted out the toy, continue the activity by asking: *Do you like (yo-yos)?* After they respond with gestures such as nodding or shaking their heads, ask the rest of the class: *Does (he/she) like (yo-yos)? Yes, (he/she) does. No, (he/she) doesn't.*

Name a Toy

Students stand in a circle. Begin by saying a student's name and throwing him or her the ball. The student catches the ball and names a toy. This student continues the game by calling out another student's name and throwing the ball. Students catch the ball and try to name different toys as they are playing. Continue until everyone has had a turn to name a toy and catch the ball. Leave the Picture Cards on the board for students to use as a reference when playing.

Vocabulary: ball(s), boat(s), car(s), crayon(s), doll(s), kite(s), puzzle(s), train(s), yo-yo(s)

Lesson Objectives
✓ to name toys
✓ to ask questions using *want*
✓ to use *Yes, I do. No, I don't.*
✓ to use singular and plural nouns

Classroom English
• Say. Write. Read. Check.

Language Patterns
• Do you want a (kite)?
• Do you like (trains)?
• Yes, I do. No, I don't.

Materials
• **Realia:** doll, yo-yo, toy train, kite, toy car, ball, puzzle, crayon(s), toy boat
• **Picture Cards:** doll, yo-yo, train, kite, car, ball, puzzle, crayon, boat

WARMING UP

Hold up the doll or the Picture Card for doll and ask the question: *Do you like (dolls)?* Gesture and nod your head. Say: *Yes, I do.* Ask students to repeat with you. Now hold up a train and say: *Do you like (trains)?* Shake your head and gesture no. Say: *No, I don't.* Students repeat.

Practice the question. Invite a student to come up. Ask the rest of the class to repeat the question: *Do you like (kites)?* The student at the front of the room gestures and either nods or shakes his or her head. Model the response and ask the student to repeat. Continue the activity, giving each student a chance to participate.

USING PAGE 74

Help students find page 74 in their books. Play the recording or read the Grammar Box with students. Ask them to follow along and read with

you. Point to the pictures as you read. Tell students that when we ask each other about likes and dislikes, we always use the plural form of the noun. Also, we can answer with a short answer: *Yes, I do.* or *No, I don't.*

Read the directions for the writing activity. Explain that they should answer the questions about themselves. Read the first question and elicit responses from students either: *Yes, I do.* or *No, I don't.* Help students check the box that answers the question so that it reflects their opinion. Students trace the words to write the question. Help students fill in the missing words and trace the rest of the question. After students have finished the page, ask the question and tell students who answered: *Yes, I do.* to stand and read their response

chorally. Repeat this for students who answered: *No, I don't.*

HAVING FUN!
Ask Around

Students sit in a circle. Hold up a toy or a Picture Card. Ask the student on your right: *Do you like (trains)?* Model the response for them if necessary: *Yes, I do.* or *No, I don't.*, and ask them to repeat. Hand the toy, card, or a different Picture Card to this student and motion for him or her to ask the student on his or her right: *Do you like (puzzles)?* Continue around the circle.

Vocabulary: ball, boat, car, crayon, doll, kite, puzzle, train, yo-yo

Lesson Objectives

✓ to name toys

✓ to ask questions using *want*

✓ to use *Yes, I do.* or *No, I don't.*

Classroom English

• Say. Write. Find. What is this? It is a (train). What are they? They are (trains).

Language Patterns

• What's this? It's a (doll).

• What are they? They are (trains).

• Do you want a (train)?

• Yes, I do. No, I don't.

Materials

• crayons; pencils; drawing paper; index cards with the words: *doll, dolls, yo-yo, yo-yos, train, trains, kite, kites, car, cars, ball, balls, puzzle, puzzles, crayon, crayons, boat, boats*

• **Realia:** doll, yo-yo, toy train, kite, toy car, ball, puzzle, crayon(s), toy boat

• **Picture Cards:** doll, kite, yo-yo, car, train, ball, puzzle, crayon, boat

WARMING UP

Hold up one Picture Card and ask: *Do you want a (doll)?* Gesture and smile to show you want the doll and respond: *Yes, I do.* Now hold up a (kite) and say: *Do you want a (kite)?* Gesture and frown to show that you don't want the kite and say: *No, I don't.* Hold up a toy or a Picture Card and ask a student: *Do you want a (yo-yo)?* Allow them to nod or shake their heads. Model the appropriate response and ask them to repeat. Continue the activity, giving each student a chance to participate.

Invite two students to come up. Give Student 1 a Picture Card or toy and model the question for him or her: *Do you want a (car)?* Student 1 asks Student 2. Student 2 gestures and answers either: *Yes, I do.* or *No, I don't.* If they respond *No, I don't.*, help students tell what they want by adding: *I want a (train).* Model responses for students if necessary.

USING PAGE 75

Help students find page 75 in their books. Play the recording or read the questions and answers. Ask students to repeat. Explain that we use the singular form of nouns when we ask what other people want. We can answer using a short answer: *Yes, I do.* or *No, I don't.* Explain that when we say: *No, I don't.* we can continue the response by telling what we want: *No, I don't. I want a (car).*

Show students a picture of a kite you have drawn ahead of time and write: *I want a (kite).* at the bottom of your paper. Ask students to identify the picture and read the sentence at the bottom of the paper.

Ask students to tell what they want and to draw a picture of it in the box. Circulate as students are working and provide help when they complete the sentence at the bottom of the page. When students are finished, ask them to share their work by saying: *I want a (car).*

USING PAGE 76

Help students find page 76 in their books. Point to number 1 and ask students to talk about the picture. Ask them to tell who and what they see. Read the question and answer with the class. Ask them to trace the words. Ask students to tell who and what they see in number 2. Read the incomplete question and ask students to tell what word is missing. Explain that Luis doesn't want the doll. Read the first word in the response and ask them to tell which words are missing. Students complete the page by writing the missing words on the lines.

HAVING FUN!
Singular and Plural Toy Words

Write the singular and plural toy words on index cards ahead of time. Draw a simple picture for each one. Hold up each card and ask students to identify the pictures and to read the words. Place the index cards facedown on the floor or table in front of students. Students take turns turning over two cards. If they find the singular and plural form of a word, they keep the pair. The student with the most pairs at the end of the game wins. Encourage students to identify the toys on the index cards and to read the words.

Toy Store

Set up the toys or the Picture Cards to look like a toy store. Begin by identifying the toys or Picture Cards with the class. Prompt students with: *What's this?* Model responses if necessary: *It's a (kite)*. Invite a student to come to the "toy store." Ask: *Do you want a (yo-yo)?* Help students respond with an affirmative or negative short answer, depending on what they want. Continue asking questions until you find out which toy he or she

Write.

1.

Do you **want** a puzzle?

Yes, I do.

2.

Do you **want** a doll?

No, I don't.

3.

Do you **want** a car?

No, I don't.

wants. Continue until everyone has had a turn. Now give students a turn to be the "shopkeeper." Students can practice asking the questions chorally before beginning. Students ask each other: *Do you want a (kite)?* and continue asking until they find the toy that the other student wants.

Listening Activity

Ask students to form a line from the front to the back of the room. Whisper to the first student: *I want a (doll)*. This student whispers it to the next student. Students continue whispering the sentence until the last student is reached. The last student asks the first student: *Do you want a (doll)?* The first student responds either: *Yes, I do.* or *No, I don't.* and

then points to the Picture Card to show what the original sentence was. Continue the activity and try to give each student a chance to be either the first or last one in line.

Vocabulary: ball, boat, car, crayons, doll, kite, puzzle, train, yo-yo

Lesson Objectives

✓ to name toys

✓ to ask questions using *want*

✓ to use *Yes, I do. No, I don't.*

✓ to tell what you like

Classroom English

• Show me. Find. Say. Do you want a (train)? Yes, I do. No, I don't.

Language Patterns

• Do you like (trains)? Yes, I do. No, I don't. I like (trains).

Materials

• paper clips

• **Realia:** doll, yo-yo, toy train, kite, toy car, ball, puzzle, crayon, toy boat

• **Picture Cards:** doll, yo-yo, train, kite, car, ball, puzzle, crayon, boat

WARM UP

Show students the Picture Cards for: *doll, yo-yo, train, kite, car, ball, puzzle, crayon, boat.* Ask them to identify each one. Ask: *What is it?* Help students respond: *It is a (puzzle).* Ask each student to tell what he or she wants. Prompt them with the question: *Do you want a (train)?* Model short answer responses: *Yes, I do. No, I don't. I want a (kite).*

USING PAGE 77

Help students find page 77 in their books. Play the recording or read the chant for them. Model and ask students to follow along and point to each word as they listen. After students have listened to and read the chant a few times, invite them to say it with you. Encourage students to point to each word as they read and then to find the corresponding picture to each stanza.

🎧 **Chant.**

Do you want,
Do you want,
Do you want a train?

Yes, yes,
Yes, I do.
Yes, I want a train!

Do you want,
Do you want,
Do you want a ball?

Yes, yes,
Yes, I do.
Yes, I want a ball.

Do you like ...?, Does he/she like ...?, Do you want ...? 77

Divide the class into two groups. Group 1 can ask the question and group 2 can say the response. Allow students to practice both parts.

EXTENSION
Continue the Chant

Review the chant with students by playing the recording or reading it for them. Substitute other toys. Hold up the toy or the Picture Card to prompt students. Students say the new chant.

USING PAGE 78

Help students find page 78 in their books. Say: *Show me a (ball). Show me a (train)*. Read the directions and model how the game is played. Toss a paper clip onto the game board. Name the toy it lands on and tell whether you like the toy or not: *Trains. I like trains.* Encourage students to express their likes and dislikes. Model responses for students, if necessary, and ask them to repeat. Remind students to use the plural form of the noun when responding.

EXTENSION
Ask and Answer

Play the game again. After the student tosses the paper clip, the rest of the students ask: *Do you like (trains)?* Then the player responds: *Yes, I do.* or *No, I don't.*

Talk about the Pictures

Play the game again and ask students to tell what they see. For example: *It's a (ball).*

Do you like ...?

Drop a paper clip onto an object in the circle.

78 UNIT 8 | In the Toy Store

Units 7 & 8
Review

Vocabulary: ball, balloon, boat, cake, camera, candy, car, card, doll, kite, numbers 1–10, present, puzzle, yo-yo

Review Objectives
✓ to talk about birthday parties
✓ to count to ten
✓ to name toys
✓ to use possessive pronouns *his* and *her*
✓ to express likes and dislikes

Classroom English
• Listen. Check. Point. Say.
• It is a (balloon). This is a (car).

Language Patterns
• This is (her) (doll).
• Does (he) like (yo-yos)? Yes. No.
• Do you like (cars)? Yes, I do. No, I don't.

Materials
• **Realia:** present, cake, candy, card, camera, yo-yo, doll, ball, toy boat, toy car, kite, balloon, puzzle
• **Picture Cards:** present, cake, candy, card, camera, yo-yo, doll, ball, boat, car, kite, balloon, puzzle

WARMING UP

Review the vocabulary words from Units 7 and 8 with students. Use the Picture Cards or realia. Ask: *What is it?* Invite students to use a complete sentence when answering: *It is a puzzle.*

Review counting from 1 to 10 with students. Write the numerals 1 to 10 on the board. Begin by counting from 1 to 10, then count backwards from 10 to 1. Ask students to close their eyes. Erase a number from the board and ask students to tell which one is missing. Draw different numbers of balloons, cars, or yo-yos on the board. Ask students to count them and to find the numeral that shows how many they see.

Review the possessive pronouns *his* and *her* with students. Invite a boy to come up to the front of the room. Ask him or her to identify and choose a Picture Card. Ask the rest of the class to tell whose (car) it is. Model responses if necessary. Repeat the activity with similar examples.

Review *he/she likes* with students. Invite a student to come up to the front of the classroom. Hand him or her a Picture Card and ask *Do you like (cars)?* Model the response if necessary: *Yes, I do.* or *No, I don't.* Then ask the rest of the class: *Does (he/she) like (cars)?* Model the

---

Review: Units 7 and 8

Vocabulary
🎧 **A. Listen and check.**

His/Her
🎧 **B. Listen and check.**

Review | Units 7 and 8   79

AUDIOSCRIPT

A. 1. yo-yo   2. doll   3. boat   4. puzzle   5. card   6. camera

B. 1. This is her kite.   2. This is her ball.   3. This is her doll.   4. This is his present.
5. This is his cake.   6. This is her balloon.

response if necessary and ask students to repeat. Continue the activity with similar examples.

If you feel students need to practice exercises that are similar to those presented in the Review Units, use exercises similar to the ones described for Review Units 1 and 2, pages 25–26. Students can practice checking boxes and pictures that go with sentences and words that are said.

USING PAGE 79

Help students find page 79 in their books. Help students find exercise A. Read the directions and ask them to follow along. Point to each picture and ask students to say the words with you. Explain that they should listen and check the picture that goes with the word that is said. Play the recording or read the audioscript for students. Students check the correct picture.

Help students find Exercise B. Read the directions and ask them to follow along. Point to the pictures and ask students to tell who the items belong to and to use *his* or *her*. Explain that students should check the *yes* or *no* box according to the sentence that is said. Play the recording or read the audioscript. Students check the correct box.

USING PAGE 80

Help students find page 80 in their books. Help students find Exercise C. Read the directions and ask them to

follow along. Explain to students that they should mark either *yes* or *no* depending on the question that is asked. Play the recording or read the audioscript for students. Students mark the correct box.

Help students find Exercise D. Read the directions and ask them to follow along. Explain that they should listen, point to the pictures, and repeat the question and the answer. Play the

recording or read the audioscript. Students repeat.

Review: Units 7 and 8

Does he/she like ...?
🎧 C. Listen and check.

Do you like ...?
🎧 D. Listen, point, and say.

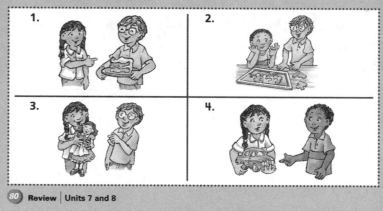

AUDIOSCRIPT

C. 1. Does he like yo-yos?   2. Does she like cars?   3. Does she like dolls?   4. Does he like cake?
   5. Does he like kites?   6. Does she like presents?

D. 1. Do you like cake? Yes I do.   2. Do you like puzzles? No I don't.
   3. Do you like dolls? Yes I do.   4. Do you like cars? No I don't.

Unit 9
Outdoor Activities

Can/Can't/Can you ...?

Vocabulary: bike, climb, fly, jump, kite, play, ride, run, soccer ball, swim, tree

Lesson Objectives
- ✓ to identify actions
- ✓ to talk about outdoor activities
- ✓ to use *can* to show ability

Classroom English
- Find. Say. Draw. Listen. Write.

Language Patterns
- (I/She/He) can (swim).

Materials
- drawing paper; crayons; bag or box; two sets of index cards with words, Set 1: *I can ride; I can play; I can climb; I can fly;* Set 2: *a bike, soccer, a tree, a kite;* index cards with words: *run, jump, climb, play, ride, swim, fly;* slips of paper with the words: *run, jump, play, soccer, swim, climb a tree, ride a bike, fly a kite*
- **Realia:** kite, soccer ball
- **Picture Cards:** run, jump, climb, play, ride, swim, fly, ball, tree, kite

WARMING UP

Bring in a soccer ball and a kite or show the Picture Cards for each word. Help students understand that we use these things when we are outdoors. Act out using each item. Students repeat: *soccer ball, kite.* Now add the verb and ask students to role-play the activity with you: *play soccer, fly a kite.*

Use Picture Cards and role playing to act out these verbs: *run, jump, climb a tree, ride a bike, swim.* As you act out each one, ask students to join you. Play the recording and have students repeat.

When students are comfortable with the new vocabulary, act out *fly a kite.* Show the Picture Card and say: *I can fly a kite.* Ask students to role-play with you and to say the sentence. Use a similar procedure to present the rest of

the verbs in sentences using *can.* Explain that we use *can* to show ability.

USING PAGE 81

Help students find page 81 in their books. Students identify who and what they see. Point to each item in the picture as you play the recording or read the words. Students repeat. Give the following directions and complete the page with students: *Draw a red circle around* run. Continue with different colors for each vocabulary word.

USING PAGE 82

Help students find page 82 in their books. Play the recording or read the Grammar Box as you point to the

pictures. Students read with you. Explain that we use *can* and an action to show the ability to do something.

Point to each picture as you read the directions for the writing activity. Students follow along. Model sentences for students: *She can run. He can climb a tree. She can jump. He can ride a bike.* Ask students to repeat.

(Continued on page 82.)

Outdoor Activities

fly a kite	climb a tree
play soccer	
run	
jump	
swim	ride a bike

Read the first sentence of the exercise with students and help them see that it goes with the first picture. Ask students to trace the words.

Point to the picture in number 2 and ask students to tell what Tom can do. Read the first two words in the sentence and help students decide which word or words best finishes the sentence. Use a similar procedure to complete numbers 3 and 4.

HAVING FUN!
Charades

Write the following activities on slips of paper ahead of time: *run, jump, play soccer, swim, climb a tree, ride a bike, fly a kite.* Read each one with students and then fold the slips of paper and place them in a box or bag.

Students choose a slip of paper, read it, and act it out. The student who guesses correctly first gets to act out the next activity. You can read and whisper the activity to students with limited English ability.

Match the Activity to the Item

Write the following words on index cards ahead of time: Set 1: *I can ride, I can play, I can climb, I can fly.* Set 2: *a bike, soccer, a tree, a kite.*

Place the Picture Cards on the floor in front of students and say: *play soccer, ride a bike, climb a tree, fly a kite.* Review sentences with *can: I can (climb a tree).* Read Set 1 with students and then ask volunteers to place index cards on the corresponding Picture Cards. Read Set 2 with students and ask volunteers to use these index cards to complete the sentences for each Picture Card. Read each sentence with students and explain that only certain words can be used to complete each sentence.

Favorite Activity

Draw a picture of your favorite activity ahead of time and label it with a sentence: *I can (swim).* Show the picture to students and explain that you like this activity. Read the sentence under your picture. Give each student a piece of drawing paper and crayons. Ask them to draw a picture of their activity and write a sentence. Circulate and offer assistance to students who need help writing a sentence under their pictures. Sentences should follow the pattern: *I can (swim).*

When students are finished, ask them to sit in a circle. Begin by showing your picture. Read your sentence: *I can (swim).* Invite students to share

their work. Students show their pictures and read the sentences they wrote.

Three in a Row

Model the activity. Place the Picture Cards on the floor in front of students or on the board. Say three activities, such as: *run, jump, swim.* Students must repeat them in the same order and then point to the corresponding Picture Cards in the correct order. Play until everyone has had a turn. Use the actions: *run, jump, play soccer, swim, climb a tree, ride a bike, fly a kite.* Students with more English ability can say sentences using *can: I can run. I can jump. I can swim.*

Vocabulary: bike, climb, jump, kite, play, ride, run, soccer ball, swim, tree

Lesson Objectives
✓ to identify actions

✓ to talk about outdoor activities

✓ to use *can* to show ability

✓ to use *can't* to show inability

✓ to use pronouns *he* and *she*

Classroom English
• Say. Write. Find. Show me. What is this? What is it? It is a (kite).

Language Patterns
• I can (play soccer).

• I can't (ride a bike).

Materials
• bingo grids with nine spaces, one for each student; bingo markers; drawing paper; crayons

• **Realia:** kite, soccer ball

• **Picture Cards:** run, jump, climb, play, ride, swim, fly, kite

WARMING UP

Hide the kite and soccer ball or the Picture Cards for these items in the classroom ahead of time. Try to make the items slightly visible to students. Ask students to sit in a circle. Begin by saying: *I can find the (kite).* Walk to the kite and show it to students. Now say: *I can't find the soccer ball. I can't.* Look around and gesture that you can't find the item or Picture Card. Ask a student to help you. After the student has found the card, say: *He can find the ball.* Use a similar procedure to practice *can* and *can't* and the actions from this lesson. You can ask students to close their eyes as you hide additional items or Picture Cards.

USING PAGE 83

Help students find page 83 in their books. Play the recording or read the

Grammar Box with students. Ask them to follow along and read with you. Point to the pictures as you read. Remind students that we use *can* plus an action to show ability. Explain that we use *can't* to show inability. Explain how the contraction *can't* is formed from *can not.*

Read the directions for the writing activity with students. Point to each picture and ask students to tell who and what they see. Ask students to say sentences for each picture, for example: *He can't play soccer.* After students have practiced saying the sentences, read the first sentence and ask them to trace the words.

For number two, ask students to tell what Maria can't do in the picture. Read the first two words in the

sentence and ask students to tell what words are missing. Ask them to write the missing words on the line. Help students write the sentences for numbers three and four.

USING PAGE 84

Begin by helping students find page 84 in their books. Read the directions for the activity with the class. Point to each picture and ask students to tell what each child can and can't do in the chart.

Now read the first sentence with students and help them read the chart. Students should point to *Maria* and *bike.* Help them see that the chart shows that Maria can ride a bike. Now read the first sentence and ask students to trace the words.

Use a similar procedure to complete the rest of the page. Help students locate the students and activity on the chart. Then have them decide which word best finishes the sentence, *can* or *can't.*

HAVING FUN!
Listening Game

The words *can* and *can't* might sound very similar to students. Play a listening game to help them discriminate between the two words. Ask students to listen carefully. Say the words in pairs. If the pair of words is the same, students stand. If the pair of words is different, they sit down. For example: *Can, can't.* Students sit. *Can, can.* Students stand.

After students have had a chance to listen to the words, invite them to say the words with you for additional practice.

Listen and Say

Ask students to stand in a line from the front to the back of the classroom. Place the Picture Cards: *run, jump, play, swim, climb, ride, fly* on the board. Say each word with students. Now whisper a sentence to the first student in line using *can* or *can't* plus one of these actions: *I can swim.* or *I can't ride.* Motion for this student to

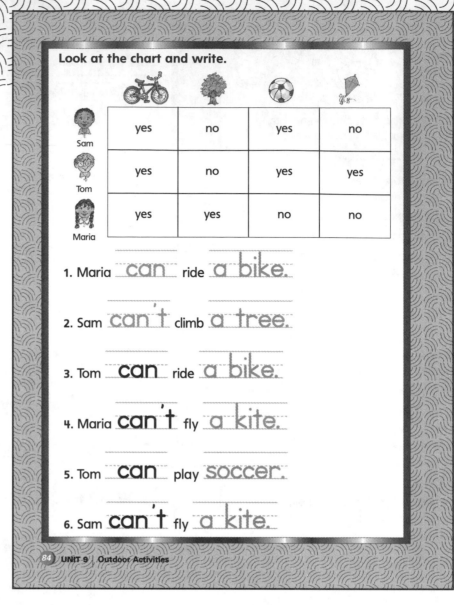

Look at the chart and write.

	🚲	🌳	⚽	🪁
Sam	yes	no	yes	no
Tom	yes	no	yes	yes
Maria	yes	yes	no	no

1. Maria <u>can</u> ride <u>a bike.</u>

2. Sam <u>can't</u> climb <u>a tree.</u>

3. Tom <u>can</u> ride <u>a bike.</u>

4. Maria <u>can't</u> fly <u>a kite.</u>

5. Tom <u>can</u> play <u>soccer.</u>

6. Sam <u>can't</u> fly <u>a kite.</u>

whisper it to the next student. Continue in this manner until the last student is reached. This student says the sentence and points to the corresponding Picture Card. The first student tells if the sentence is correct. Try to give each student a chance to be either the first or last in line.

Action Bingo

Prepare bingo grids with nine spaces for each student. Use paper clips or small pieces of paper for markers. Give each student a grid. Tell students that everyone's bingo grid should be different, and to draw their pictures in any space on the paper. Students write the word *free* in the center box. Students should draw and label the following words and phrases: *run,*

jump, play ball, swim, climb a tree, ride a bike, fly a kite. Call out a phrase. Students place markers on the pictures. Three in a row wins. The winner reads his or her winning words and uses them in a sentence with the word *can: I can (ride a bike).*

I Can and I Can't

This game is played like Simon Says. Say sentences using the actions plus *can* and *can't.* When you use *can,* students do the action. When you say *can't,* students do nothing. For example: *I can (jump).* Students jump. *I can't swim.* Students do nothing.

Vocabulary: climb a tree, fly a kite, jump, play soccer, ride a bike, run, swim

Lesson Objectives
✓ to identify actions

✓ to talk about outdoor activities

✓ to use *can* to show ability

✓ to use *can't* to show inability

✓ to use *Yes, (I/he/she) can.* and *No, (I/he/she) can't.*

Classroom English
• Show me. Write. Draw. Put. Find. Listen. Say. Simon Says. What is this? What is it? It's a (soccer ball).

Language Patterns
• Can you (swim)?

• Can (he/she) (fly a kite)?

• Yes, (I/he/she) can. No, (I/he/she) can't.

Materials
• hole punch; yarn or string; a boy and a girl puppet; *can* and *can't* on slips of paper, paper bag, drawing paper, crayons

• **Realia:** soccer ball

• **Picture Cards:** run, jump, play, swim, climb, ride, fly

WARMING UP

Use puppets for this activity. You can make them with old socks or construction paper. Make one boy and one girl. Hold up a puppet and point to the Picture Card: *(fly)*. Ask the puppet: *Can you (fly a kite)?* The puppet gestures *yes* and says: *Yes, I can.* Students practice asking the question with you and then ask the puppet. The puppet responds either: *Yes, I can.* or *No, I can't.* Now invite a student to come up and ask the boy puppet: *Can you (ride a bike)?* The puppet responds: *Yes, I can.* Now ask the students: *Can he (ride a bike)?* Model the response: *Yes, he can.* Ask students to repeat.

Use a similar procedure for *she*, using the girl puppet. Ask individual students questions as you show Picture Cards: *Can you (swim)?* Ellicit answers: *Yes, I can. No, I can't.*

USING PAGE 85

Help students find page 85 in their books. Ask students to tell who they see and what the action is. Play the recording or read the Grammar Box for students as they follow along. Point to the picture as you read. Students repeat. Explain that we can ask about each other's abilities by asking the question: *Can you (swim)?* and then use a short answer to respond: *Yes, I can.* to show ability and *No, I can't.* to show inability.

Read the directions for the exercise with students. Show students the Picture Card *run* and read the question with them. Read both possible answers and ask students to read with you. Students check the box that applies to them. When finished, students can ask each other the questions.

USING PAGE 86

Help students find page 86 in their books. Play the recording or read the Grammar Box as students follow along. Point to each picture as you read. Ask the class to read chorally. Explain that we can ask about someone else's ability by using questions with *can* and an action. Remind students that *he* is used for men and boys and *she* is used for women and girls.

Read the directions for the writing activity. Ask students to talk about the pictures using *can*. Point to number 1 and ask students to tell what question should go on the line. Elicit the question: *Can he ride a bike?* and have students write it. Use a similar procedure to complete the page.

HAVING FUN!
A Verb Picture Dictionary

Make a verb picture dictionary with students. Give each student eight pieces of drawing paper. Show them how to make a cover for their dictionaries with the title: *I Can.* Ask them to draw one picture at a time with you. Write the action words on the board for students to use as a reference when writing a label for their pictures. Students can draw pictures for these words: *run, jump, play soccer, swim, climb a tree, ride a bike, fly a kite*. Provide assistance for students when they need to assemble their dictionaries. Punch holes in their papers and tie them with yarn or string. When they are finished, invite individuals to share their dictionaries with the class.

Act Out *Can* and *Can't* with Actions

Write the word *can* on five slips of paper and the word *can't* on five slips of paper. Fold the papers and place them in a paper bag. Place the Picture Cards facedown on the table. Model the activity. Students choose

a Picture Card and a slip of paper from the bag. They act out *can* or *can't* plus the activity. The rest of the students guess the activity. For example: *He can't climb a tree. He can swim.* The student who guesses correctly first gets to be the next actor.

Name an Outdoor Activity

Place the Picture Cards on the board for students to use as a reference while playing. Use a soccer ball. Throw the soccer ball to a student. The student catches the soccer ball, names an action, and acts it out. He or she then throws the soccer ball to another student who names a different action and acts it out. Students should call out the name of

the person they are throwing the ball to. Play until everyone has had a turn. Encourage students to name different actions while playing and to include sentences such as: *I can (swim).*

Vocabulary: bike, climb, fly, jump, kite, play, ride, run, soccer ball, swim, tree

WARMING UP

Begin by reviewing the actions from this lesson. Hold up a Picture Card and ask students to identify the activity by saying the verb. Then ask individual students: *Can you (run)?* as you hold up the corresponding Picture Card. Ask students to answer the question about themselves. Students answer using a short answer: *Yes, I can. No, I can't.*

USING PAGE 87

Help students find page 87 in their books. Play the recording or read the chant for students. Act out each action as it appears in the chant. Model and ask students to follow along and point to each word as they listen. After students have listened to and read the chant a few times, invite them to say it with you. Encourage them to point to each word as they read and to act out the actions with you.

🎧 **Chant.**

Can you run?

Yes, I can.

Yes, I can.

Can you swim?

Yes, I can.

Yes, I can.

Can you jump?

Yes, I can.

Yes, I can.

Can/Can't/Can ...? 87

EXTENSION
Continue the Chant

Review the chant with students by playing the recording or reading it for them. Substitute other activities or actions. Students say the new chant and act out the new action. Point to individual students to answer the question about themselves.

Using Page 88

Show students two completed pictures of activities you can do. Write sentences under each picture: *I can (swim). I can (run).* Ask students to identify the actions and to read the sentences with you. Help students find page 88 in their books. Ask them to draw two pictures that show what they can do. Circulate as students work and help them fill in the action word or activity.

Extension

Invite students to come up to the front of the room with their pictures. Ask them to name the action and to read the completed sentences to the rest of the class.

Information Gap Activity

Ask students to sit back-to-back. Students hide their pictures from their partners. Students ask each other questions to discover what pictures their partner has drawn. For example:

Student 1: *Can you (swim)?*
Student 2: *Yes, I can. No, I can't.*

Draw 2 things you can do. Then write.

1.

I can _____.

2.

I can _____.

Unit 10
Food

Present Progressive, *How many ...?*

Vocabulary: bake, banana, cake, cookie, drink, eat, grapes, hamburger, hot dog, juice, milk, wash

Lesson Objectives
✓ to name foods
✓ to use the present progressive

Classroom English
• Find. Say. Draw. Listen. Write. Show me. What is this? What is it?
• It is a (cookie). It is (milk). What are they? They are (grapes).

Language Patterns
• I am (eating). What are you doing?
• What is this? What is it?
• It is (milk). It is a (cookie).

Materials
• drawing paper; crayons; big bag or box; sentences written on slips of paper; two large paper bags labeled *A* and *No A*
• **Realia:** grapes, cookies, bananas
• **Picture Cards:** hamburger, grapes, cookie, milk, cake, juice, banana, hot dog, eat, drink, bake, wash

Food

bananas hot dog cookies cake grapes drink milk juice hamburger

WARMING UP

Show students the food Picture Cards or realia and say each word for them. Ask students to repeat. When they are familiar with the new vocabulary, model sentences such as: *It is a (cookie). It is (milk).* Students will be working with mass and count words in this unit. Model each kind of sentence and allow as much practice as possible. When students make a mistake, correct them by modeling the correct answer. Students are not expected to master this concept at this time.

Show students the hamburger Picture Card and act out eating. Say: *I am eating a hamburger.* Use a similar procedure for: *grapes, cookie, banana, cake, hot dog.* Ask students

to repeat. Use a similar procedure for *I am drinking (milk, juice); I am baking cookies;* and *I am washing the dishes.*

Invite a student to come up, choose a verb Picture Card and a food Picture Card. Students act out. For example, *eating/bananas.* Students act out: *I am eating bananas.* Model the question and practice saying it with students: *What are you doing?* The student responds: *I am eating bananas.* Continue until everyone has had a chance to participate.

USING PAGE 89

Help students find page 89 in their books. Play the recording or read, point to each food, and ask students

to listen and repeat. Use complete sentences: *It is a (cookie). It is (milk).* Point to the people in the picture and ask what they are doing. Accept one word answers: *washing, eating, drinking.*

Give the following directions and complete the page with students: *Draw a yellow circle around the bananas. Draw a red circle around eating.* Continue with different colors for each of the words.

USING PAGE 90

Help students find page 90 in their books. Play the recording or read the Grammar Box as you point to the picture. Students read with you. Explain that we can ask and tell what is happening now by using questions and answers like the ones presented here.

Read the directions for the writing activity. Students follow along. Ask students to tell what each person is doing. Read the first question and answer with students and help them see that it goes with the first picture. Read the question and answer with students and ask them to trace the words to write the question. Help students to write the complete questions and read the answers for numbers two, three, and four.

HAVING FUN!
Act It Out

Place the food Picture Cards and the verb Picture Cards on the floor or on the board. Students choose a food and a verb, but don't tell the class which ones they chose. Students then act out the action, using the food they chose. The student who guesses correctly first gets to be the next actor.

What are you doing?

Write the following sentences on slips of paper ahead of time: *I am eating (a hamburger, grapes, a cookie, a hot dog, cake, a banana). I am drinking (juice, milk). I am baking cookies. I am washing the dishes.* Read each sentence with students. Fold each slip of paper and place in a paper bag or box. Students choose a slip of paper and act out the sentence. The class asks: *What are you doing?* The student replies: *I am (eating a cookie).* Read and whisper sentences to students with less language ability.

What are you doing?

> What are you doing?

> I am baking cookies.

Write the questions.

1.
What are you doing?
I am washing the dishes.

2.
What are you doing?
I am eating a hot dog.

3.
What are you doing?
I am drinking milk.

4.
What are you doing?
I am baking a cake.

Sorting Mass/Count Nouns

Write *A* and *No A* on two separate paper bags. Explain that some of the food words in this unit do not use the word *a*. Model these sentences and practice before playing: *I am eating cake. I am drinking juice. I am drinking milk. I am eating a (cookie, hamburger, grape, hot dog, banana).* We say: *I am baking a cake. I am eating cake.* Do not use plurals for this game.

Hold up one of the Picture Cards and ask individual students to act out drinking or eating the food: *hamburger, grapes, cookie, milk, cake, hot dog, juice, banana.* After a student acts it out, ask him or her to put it in the correct bag, *A* or *No A.* Allow the rest of the class to help

decide if the student did this correctly. Continue until all the cards have been sorted.

Favorite Food

Draw a picture of your favorite food. Show it to students and act out eating or drinking it: *I am eating a (cookie).* Ask students to draw and color a picture of their favorite food. When they are finished, ask them to sit in a circle. Students hold up their picture and then act out eating or drinking it. The rest of the class asks: *What are you doing?* The student replies: *I am (eating) (a banana).*

Vocabulary: bake, banana, cake, cookie, drink, eat, grapes, hamburger, hot dog, juice, milk, wash

Lesson Objectives
✓ to name foods
✓ to use the present progressive

Classroom English
• Say. Write. Find. Show me. What is this? What is it? It is a (kite). What are they? They are (grapes).

Language Patterns
• What is he/she doing? He/She is (eating) (cookies).

• What are you doing? I am (baking) (cookies).

• What are they? They are (grapes).

• What is this? It is a (cookie). It is (milk).

Materials
• boy and girl puppets; two large paper bags labeled: *Nouns* and *Verbs*; magazines; scissors; glue; paper

• **Realia:** cookies, bananas, grapes

• **Picture Cards:** hamburger, grapes, cookie, milk, cake, juice, banana, hot dog, eat, drink, bake, wash

WARMING UP

Use boy and girl puppets for this activity. You can make puppets from construction paper or old socks. Hold up the boy puppet and the cookies and act out *eating cookies.* Ask: *What is he doing?* Students practice asking the question with you. Reply: *He is eating cookies.* Use a similar procedure when presenting sentences with *she.* Give students a chance to practice asking and answering questions using the food words and verbs in this lesson and the subject pronouns: *he* and *she.*

USING PAGE 91

Help students find page 91 in their books. Play the recording or read the Grammar Box with students. Ask them to follow along and read with you. Point to the pictures as you read. Explain to students that we can ask questions about what other people are doing now by using questions and answers in the present progressive tense. When we use *he* and *she* we use the helping word *is* + an action with *-ing* at the end.

Read the directions for the writing activity. Ask students to tell who they see in the picture and to identify the verb. Read the question and answer with students and ask them to trace the words to write the question and answer. Help students fill in the missing words to complete the question in number 2. Then help them answer the question about the picture. Ask them to trace the words and help them complete the answer. Use a similar procedure to complete the page. Read each completed question and answer with students.

USING PAGE 92

Help students find page 92 in their books. Read the directions for Activity A with them. Read the words in the parentheses and ask students if these words make a sentence. Elicit that the words do not make sentences. Tell students to trace the sentence on the line. Explain that students need to add *is* and *-ing* to the verb to make sentences. Use a similar procedure to complete numbers 2 and 3, with students writing the sentence.

Read the directions for Activity B with students. Ask them to tell what action is taking place in number 1. Elicit that the action is *washing the dishes* and then ask: *What are you doing?* Students repeat. Read the answer and ask students to trace the letters to write the question.

Use a similar procedure to complete the exercise. Students talk about the action in the picture, read the answer, and write the question.

HAVING FUN!
What's Missing?

Place the food Picture Cards on the board or on the floor in front of students. Ask students to identify each food by saying a complete sentence: *It is a (cookie).* Now ask students to close their eyes. Take one Picture Card away. Students open their eyes and tell which Picture Card is missing. The student who guesses correctly first gets to take away the next card.

Sorting Nouns and Verbs

Place two large paper bags on the floor in front of students. Label the first bag *Nouns* and the second bag *Verbs*. Remind students that nouns name a person, place, or thing and verbs show action. Place the Picture Cards from this unit in a pile. Ask

A. Write sentences.

1. (He / eat / a hot dog)

He is eating a hot dog.

2. (She / drink / juice)

She is drinking juice.

3. (I / bake / cookies)

I am baking cookies.

B. Write the questions.

1.

What are you doing?

I am washing the dishes.

2.

What is he doing?

He is eating a hamburger.

3.

What is she doing?

She is baking cookies.

92   UNIT 10   Food

students to name each food or to tell what the action is. Invite a student to come up, choose a card, and place it in the correct bag. Encourage students to say sentences about the Picture Cards: *I am eating a banana. I am drinking milk. It is a cookie. They are grapes.* Continue until all the Picture Cards have been sorted.

Food Collages

Bring in old magazines for students to cut up. Divide the students into groups of three or four. Students cut out pictures of different food and people eating. Students glue the pictures to make collages. Students with more language ability can write labels and sentences about the pictures. As students are working,

circulate and ask questions such as: *What is this? What is he/she doing?* When collages are finished, invite students to share them with the class. Model presenting a collage by showing them a finished one you have prepared ahead of time. Use sentences such as: *He is eating cookies. She is baking cookies. This is a hot dog.*

Vocabulary: bake, banana, cake, cookie, drink, eat, grapes, hamburger, hot dog, juice, milk, wash

Lesson Objectives
✓ to name foods
✓ to use *how many*
✓ to count from 1–15

Classroom English
• Show me. Write. Draw. Find. Listen. Say. What is this? What is it? It is a (cookie). It's (milk). What are they? They are (grapes).

Language Patterns
• How many (hot dogs) do you want?
• I want (4) (hot dogs).

Materials
• numbers 1–15 written on index cards; drawing paper; scissors; crayons; purple construction paper; yellow construction paper
• **Realia:** bananas, grapes, cookies
• **Picture Cards:** hamburger, grapes, cookie, milk, cake, juice, banana, hot dog, eat, drink, bake, wash

WARMING UP

Write the numbers 1–15 on index cards ahead of time. Show students the numbers and practice counting from 1–15. Draw different numbers of bananas, cookies, or grapes on the board and count them with students. Invite a student to find the number that goes with the picture on the board.

Draw and cut out fifteen grapes from purple paper and fifteen bananas from yellow paper. Count them with students. Ask: *How many grapes do you want?* Invite a student to come up and count out the number of grapes he or she wants. Model the sentence: *I want (5) (grapes).* Ask students to practice saying it with you. Use a similar procedure to practice the other action words and foods in this unit.

Write the questions and answers on the board for students to practice reading. Invite students to trace the words of the questions and answers.

USING PAGE 93

Help students find page 93 in their books. Ask students to tell who they see and to count the hamburgers. Play the recording or read the Grammar Box with students. Point to the picture as you read. Ask the class to read chorally. Explain that when we ask questions with *how many* we are asking about the number of items. When we answer, we use a number.

Read the directions for the activity. Students repeat. Read the first question and answer with students.

Ask students to trace the words of the question. Point to the picture of the hot dogs. Ask students how many hot dogs they see. Elicit *three*. Read the answer with students. Point to the question in number 2. Ask students which words are missing. Help them to fill in *How many*. Use the procedure from number 1 to read the answers. Complete the exercise with students.

Read the questions and answers with students.

USING PAGE 94

Help students find page 94 in their books. Point to the hamburgers and ask students to tell you how many there are. Now read the question and answer and ask students to read with you. Help them see that the question and answer go with the drawing.

Read the next question. Students repeat. Ask them to draw the number of grapes they want in the box. Students write the answers about themselves. Use a similar procedure to complete the page.

HAVING FUN!
Let's Go Shopping

Ask students to draw and cut out various amounts of food items (from one through fifteen of each). Provide examples for: *grapes, cookies, hot dogs, bananas, hamburgers.* Set up part of your classroom to look like a supermarket. Students practice the conversation and then role-play being the customer and the storekeeper.

Storekeeper: *What do you want?*

Customer: *I want cookies.*

Storekeeper: *How many cookies do you want?*

Customer: *I want 4 cookies.*

Storekeeper: *(Gives customer 4 cookies.)*

Drawing Dictation

Ask students to draw food items: *Draw five grapes, ten bananas, three cookies, four hamburgers, eight hot dogs.* When students are finished, ask them to write the correct number under each picture. Point to each picture and ask: *How many (cookies) do you want?* Students answer according to the drawing: *I want 3 cookies.* When students are comfortable answering the question, practice asking the question with

them. Students can then work in pairs asking and answering: *How many (hot dogs) do you want? I want 8 hot dogs.*

Match the Number to the Picture

Draw and cut out pictures of food items: *grapes, bananas, cookies, hamburgers, hot dogs.* Use the numbers 1–15. Write the numbers 1–15 on index cards. Place each set of pictures in a pile. Invite students to come up and count the pictures. Then ask them to find the index card that shows how many food items there are in the pile. Continue the activity by asking: *How many (cookies) do you want?* Students answer and count out the number of

(cookies) they want: *I want (4) cookies.*

Act Out: Three in a Row

Model the activity for students. Say three actions. Students say and act out the actions in the order in which you said them. For example: *I am eating bananas. I am washing. I am baking cookies.* For students with more language ability, ask: *What are you doing?* Encourage them to answer using three complete sentences.

Write the answers and draw.

1. How many hamburgers do you want?

I want 5 hamburgers.

2. How many grapes do you want?

I want 13 grapes.

3. How many bananas do you want?

I want 4 bananas.

4. How many cookies do you want?

I want 10 cookies.

Vocabulary: bake, banana, cake, cookie, drink, eat, grapes, hamburger, hot dog, juice, milk, wash

Lesson Objectives
✓ to name foods
✓ to use the present progressive

Classroom English
• Draw. Show me. Find. Say. What is it? What is this? It is a (banana). It is (milk). Write. What are they? They are (cookies).

Language Patterns
• What are you doing? I am eating (bananas).
• Find the (bananas).

Materials
• Crayons; pencils or markers
• **Picture Cards:** hamburger, grapes, cookie, milk, cake, juice, banana, hot dog, eat, drink, bake, wash

WARMING UP

Review the food words and actions from this lesson. Hold up a Picture Card and ask students to identify the activity by saying the verb. Hold up a food card and ask students to tell what it is. Place the Picture Cards on the board and ask students to take turns acting out the actions along with the food words. The rest of the students can guess what is being acted out.

USING PAGE 95

Help students find page 95 in their books. Play the recording or read the chant for students. Act out each action as it appears in the chant. Model and ask students to follow along and point to each word as they listen. After students have listened to and read the chant a few times, invite them to say it with you. Encourage them to point to each word as they read and act out the actions with you. Encourage individual

🎧 **Chant.**

What are you doing?
What are you doing?

I am eating bananas.
I am eating bananas.

What are you doing?
What are you doing?

I am eating hamburgers.
I am eating hamburgers.

What are you doing?
What are you doing?

I am eating grapes.
I am eating grapes.

Present Progressive, *How many ...?* 95

students to answer using complete sentences in the present progressive tense. Model as necessary.

EXTENSION
Continue the Chant

Review the chant with students by playing the recording or reading it for them. Substitute other actions and food words. Students say the new chant and act out the new activity or action. Point to individual students to answer the question about themselves.

Take the Parts

Divide the class into two groups. One group can ask the question and the other group can answer. Model as necessary.

USING PAGE 96

Show students the picture on page 96. Say: *Find the (bananas). Circle the bananas.* Use a similar procedure for the rest of the page. Students find two bananas, three cookies, one hot dog, two cakes.

EXTENSION

How Many?

Invite students to come up to the front of the room with their pictures from page 96. Ask them to tell how many food items they see.

Color

Ask students to color the pictures: *yellow bananas, brown cookies, brown hot dogs, yellow cake.*

Find and color.

2 bananas   3 cookies   1 hot dog   2 cakes

Units 9 & 10
Review

Vocabulary: banana, cake, climbing, cookie, drinking, eating, grapes, hamburgers, hot dog, juice, jumping, making, milk, playing, riding, running, swimming

Review Objectives
✓ to identify actions
✓ to talk about outdoor activities
✓ to use *can* to show ability
✓ to name foods
✓ to use present progressive to tell what is happening now
✓ to ask and answer questions using present progressive

Classroom English
• Listen. Check. Color. Point. Say. What is it? What are they? It is a (cookie). They are (grapes).

Language Patterns
• (I/She/He) can (swim).
• I am (eating).
• What are you doing?
• What is this? What is it?
• It is (milk). It is a (cookie).

Materials
• **Realia:** soccer ball, kite, grapes, cookies, banana, cake, juice
• **Picture Cards:** hot dog, banana, cookie, juice, cake, milk, grapes, hamburger, ride, jump, wash, eat, run, swim, drink, climb, play

WARMING UP

Review the vocabulary words form Units 9 and 10 with students. Use the Picture Cards or realia. Ask: *What is it?* Invite students to use a complete

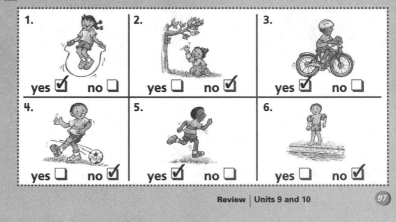

sentence when answering: *It is a (cookie).* Ask students to identify the actions: *running, eating, swimming, jumping, drinking, riding a bike, climbing a tree, playing soccer, and washing,* as you hold up the corresponding Picture Card. Model sentences such as: *He is (eating).*

Review numerals 1–10 with students by asking them to count from 1–10 and from 10–1. Then ask: *How many (cookies) do you want?* Invite a

student to come up to the board. Ask him or her to draw the number of (cookies) he or she wants and to answer: *I want (3) (cookies).* Model the response if necessary. Repeat the activity with other examples.

Act out one of the verbs and say: *I can (ride a bike).* Ask students to act it out with you and to repeat. Now act out another sentence: *I can't (swim).* Ask students to act it out with you and to repeat. Use a similar procedure for other verbs from these units.

Review present progressive verbs with students. Act out one of the verbs and ask students to act it out with you. Ask: *What are you doing?* Model the response if necessary and ask them to repeat: *I am (climbing a tree).* Repeat for the other verbs from Units 9 and 10.

If you feel students need to practice exercises that are similar to those presented in the Review Units, use exercises similar to the ones described for Review Units 1 and 2, pages 25–26. Students can practice checking boxes and pictures that go with sentences and words they hear.

USING PAGE 97

Help students find page 97 and Exercise A in their books. Read the directions and ask students to follow along. Point to each picture and ask students to say the words with you. Explain that they should listen and check the picture that goes with the word they hear. Play the recording or read the audioscript for students. Students check the correct picture.

Help students find Exercise B. Point to the pictures and ask students to tell whether the boy or girl can or can't do the action. Explain that students should check either the *yes* or *no* box depending on the sentence they hear. Play the recording or read the audioscript. Students check the correct box.

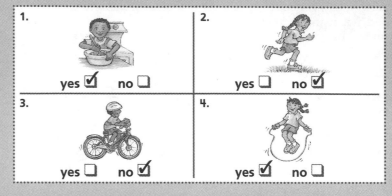

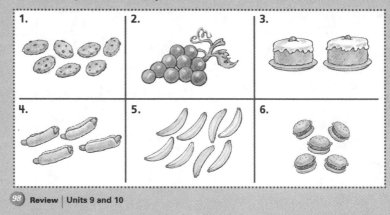

USING PAGE 98

Help students find page 98 in their books. Help students find Exercise C. Read the directions and ask them to follow along. Point to the picture in number 1 and ask students what the boy is doing. Explain that students should check either the *yes* or *no* box depending on the sentence they hear.

Play the recording or read the audioscript for students. Students mark the correct picture.

Help students find Exercise D. Read the directions and ask them to follow along. Explain that they should listen, point to the pictures, and say the sentences. Play the recording or read the audioscript. Students repeat.

AUDIOSCRIPT

C. 1. What is he doing? He is baking a cake.

    3. What is he doing? He is climbing a tree.

    2. What is she doing? She is swimming.

    4. What is she doing? She is jumping.

D. 1. How many cookies do you want? I want seven cookies.

    3. How many cakes do you want? I want two cakes.

    5. How many bananas do you want? I want eight bananas.

    2. How many grapes do you want? I want ten grapes.

    4. How mant hot dogs do you want? I want four hot dogs.

    6. How many hamburgers do you want? I want five hamburgers.

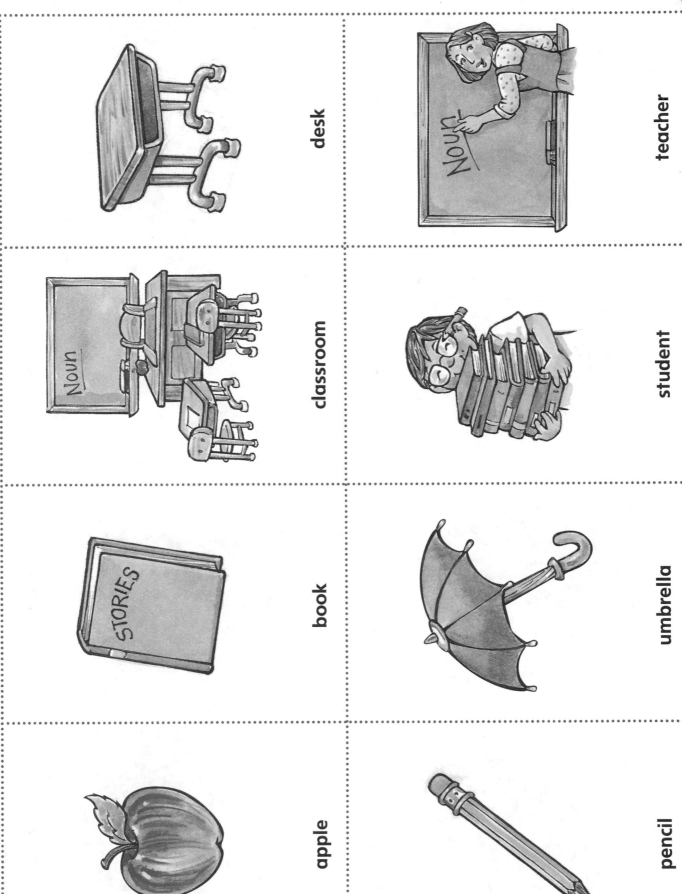

desk

teacher

classroom

student

book

umbrella

apple

pencil

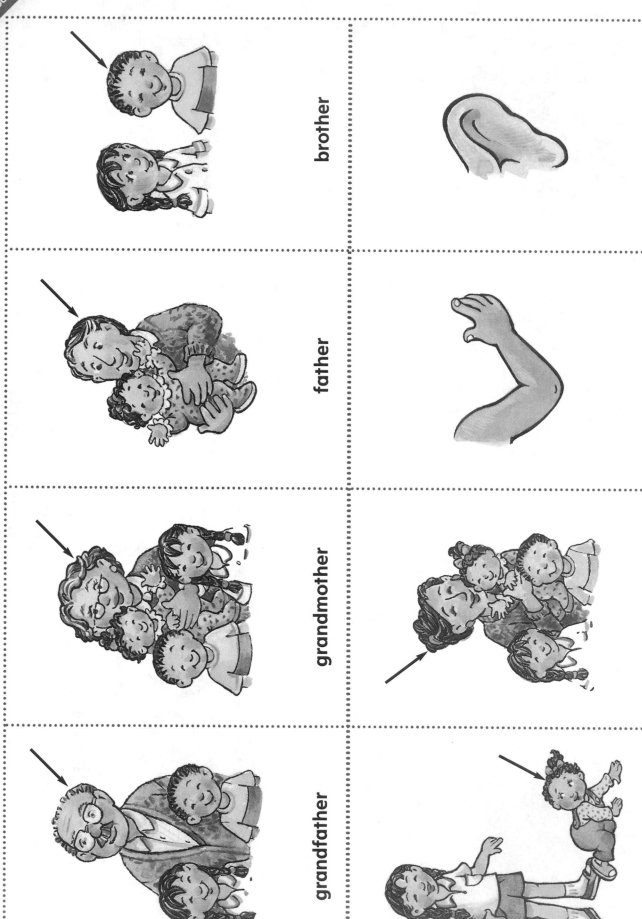

brother

ear

father

arm

grandmother

mother

grandfather

sister

nose

dress

eye

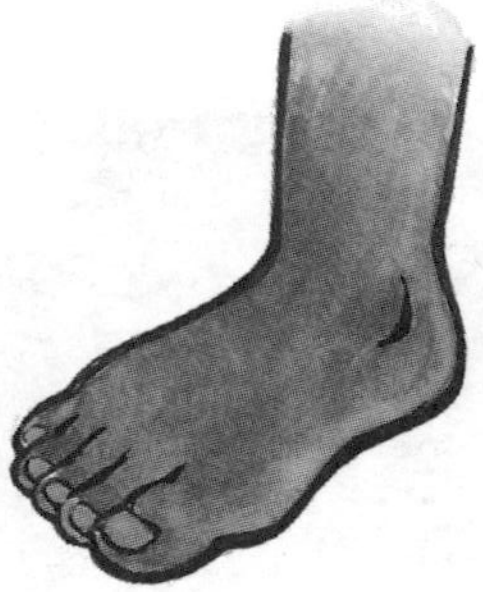

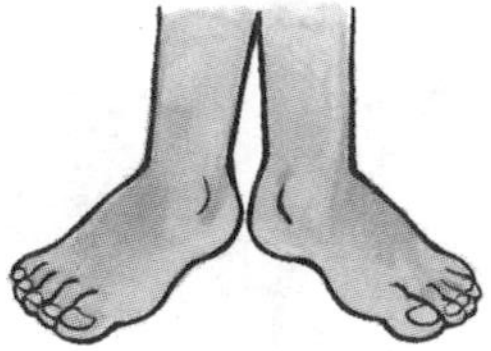

leg

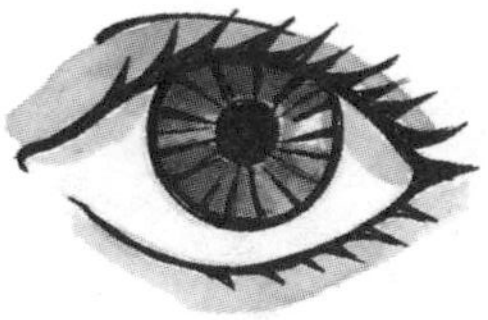

feet

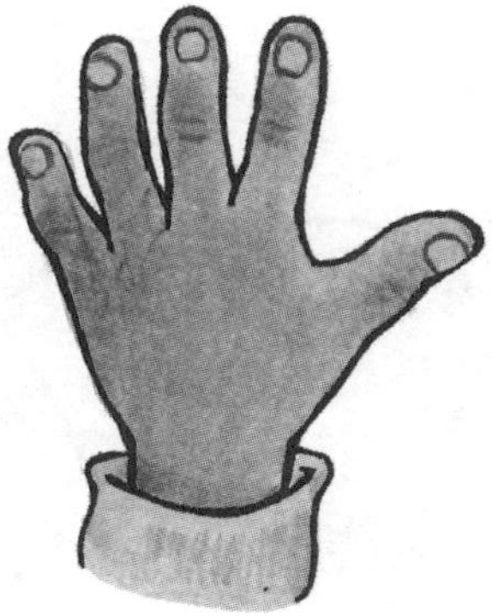

mouth

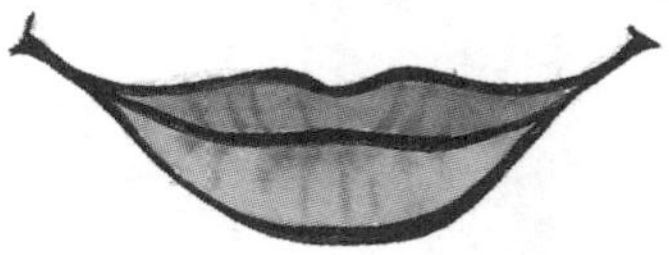

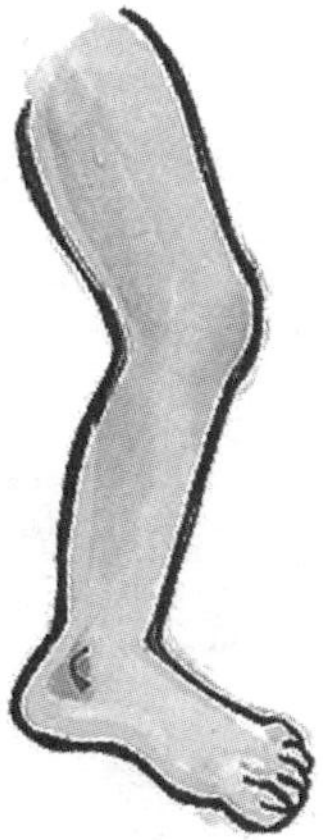

foot

hand

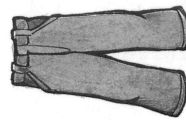

pants

coat

shoe

hat

shirt

sock

skirt

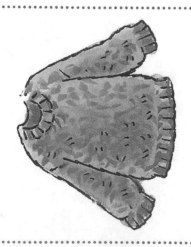

sweater

bedroom

bed

box

clock

lamp

living room

kitchen

bathroom

tub

watch

picture

read

table

sleep

chair

eat

fish

snake

frog

rabbit

bird

mouse

cat

turtle

candle

ice cream

candy

present

card

balloon

cake

camera

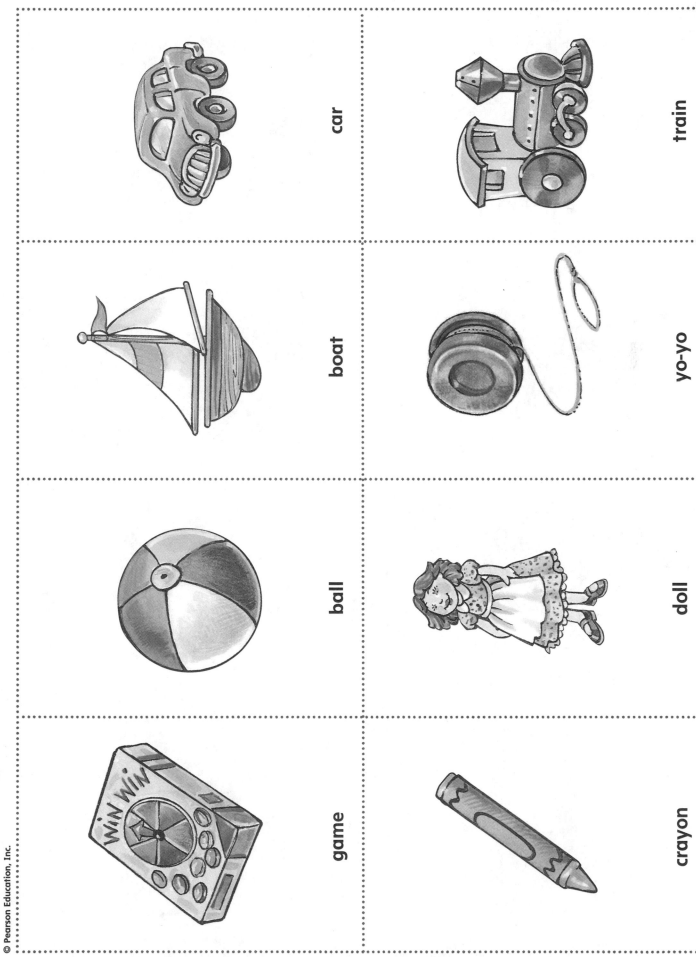

car

train

boat

yo-yo

ball

doll

game

crayon

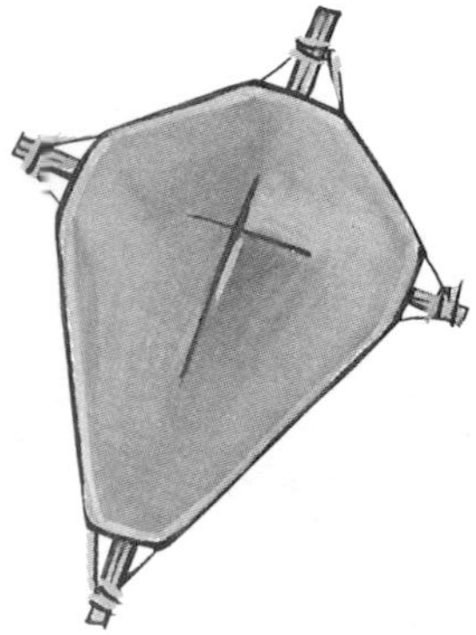

swim

climb

run

jump

puzzle

play

kite

ride

wash

juice

bake

hot dog

drink

milk

fly

hamburger

cake

tree

cookie

school

grapes

girl

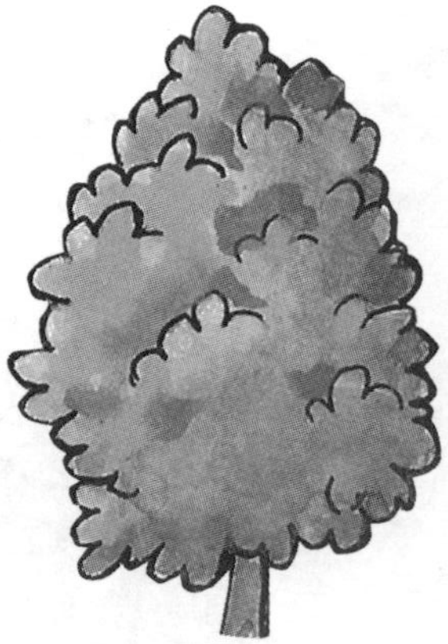

banana

boy